The Student's Music Library—Historical and Critical Studies

Edited by Percy M. Young, M.A., Mus.D.

THE VIOLIN FAMILY

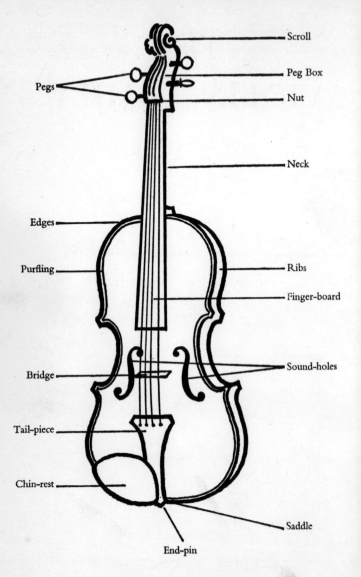

Scroll

Peg Box

Nut

Pegs

Neck

Edges

Purfling

Ribs

Finger-board

Sound-holes

Bridge

Tail-piece

Chin-rest

Saddle

End-pin

I. PARTS OF THE VIOLIN

THE
VIOLIN FAMILY

by

Sheila M. Nelson
B. Mus. (Lond.), A.R.C.M.
L.R.A.M.

LONDON: DENNIS DOBSON

Made and Printed in Great Britain by C. Tinling & Co. Ltd.
Liverpool, London and Prescot.

CONTENTS

ILLUSTRATIONS

FOREWORD

by

FRANK HOWES

If I declare my interest in this book it will not preclude me from commending it, first to all who do not play stringed instruments, and second to all who do. It contains within its ten succinct chapters a great deal of well-arranged information, much of it not common knowledge among musicians, nor even among string players, still less among non-performing devotees of music.

Those of us who do not play a stringed instrument are aware that there is a sort of freemasonry among those who do based on arcane knowledge, from which we are excluded. String players on the other hand, absorbed with their technical studies and their artistic careers, are unable to tell us some of the things we would like to know about fiddles—how, for instance, did it happen that in the middle of the eighteenth century the string quartet displaced the trio sonata and what had the viola been doing all the time?

This particular patch of fog in musical history had long bothered me when Miss Nelson came to work with me for her Bachelor of Music degree and to tackle that question of egg-or-hen priority, which London University puts into its syllabus in the form of an optional special subject, the reciprocal relation of instrumental developments and composers' demands, to which she refers on page 10. As we worked on I became aware that our roles had tacitly been reversed.

The pupil, an able violinist experienced in concerto, sonata and quartet, was now the instructor. It seemed a pity, therefore, that the copious knowledge she had acquired not only *of*, but also *about*, her instrument should be wasted on a parcel of examiners, however eminent, when it might be made available in this lucid form to anyone who is curious about the violin family but seeks in vain for some simple answers to simple questions.

FRANK HOWES.

INTRODUCTION

The violin family (violin, viola, violoncello, double bass) holds a pre-eminent position in classical music today. It contains three solo instruments which have an unrivalled ability to blend or dominate at will. It forms the basis of the symphony orchestra, can stand unsupported as a string orchestra, and plays a major part in most chamber ensembles.

Considerable research has been made, from various points of view, into how and why the members of the family have gained this important position in Western music. The aim of this book is to give a brief survey of the discoveries made in different fields. Many of them are of practical use to performer, conductor and composer; most are of interest to anyone who plays, teaches, or is otherwise connected with string music.

From the earliest appearance of a leaping violin idiom unlike the smooth, contrapuntal viol writing, music for the violin family shows considerable development in technical range and individuality : violin first, cello next, then the viola and to a more limited extent the double bass. This progress can be traced through the lives and works of leading violinists and composers, while contemporaneous advances in bow and violin construction have been noted from those instruments which remain, or from paintings and illustrations. Pictures such as the thirteenth-century drawing of Reinmar the Fiddler and published tutors like that of Francesco Geminiani also give valuable guidance as to how instruments were held and played.

The origin of the family's present shape and structure is obscure, but most of its characteristics had appeared previously in a shorter-lived stringed instrument: these details are considered individually. Only information strictly relevant to the music of the violin family has been included: for the more theoretical and mathematical aspects of string acoustics, for instance, or for details of music for viols, the reader must look elsewhere. No attempt is made to cover even the main repertoire of any instrument, but it is hoped that enough actual music is mentioned to make each chapter of the book of practical interest to musician and music-lover.

I. THE EMERGENCE OF THE VIOLIN FAMILY

A general strike of string players today would disrupt not only most classical music, including symphony concerts, chamber music and recitals, but most light music and many theatre performances. The public would be left with bands—military, jazz, brass or accordion—and with vocal ensembles: soon they would take refuge in string recordings.

The main reason for this pre-eminent position of the bowed string is probably its variety of both tone and rhythmic impetus. Any group of wind instruments has a sameness of tone which wearies the ear after a time: it has rhythmic vitality, but of a kind which seems stereotyped by comparison with the infinite grading of staccato, accent and nuance obtainable from a string orchestra or quartet. The violin family has become of the first importance to Western music because it excels in producing tone which may blend or dominate, but which does not tire the ear, and it is the most flexible and varied single medium for the composer. Over many centuries, stringed instruments were produced which possessed some of these qualities: the violin family, emerging quite late (*c.* 1550), ousted all rivals because it possessed them all.

The history of stringed instruments can be taken back to the twanging bow of a savage—bows with attached gourds as resonators are still used by primitive peoples. Plucked strings and instruments with strings struck by hammers are frequently mentioned in the Bible, but the bowed string appeared in Europe at a far later date. Leopold Mozart's suggestion that Mercury invented stringed instruments, Sappho bowing, and Orpheus the violin, would appear to be picturesque but, apart from anything else, anachronistic. Neither the ancient Greeks nor the Romans possessed a bow, in spite of the saying that Nero fiddled while Rome burned.

Bowing probably arose in the East, and was introduced into Europe during the Islamic conquests, but there is a lack of convincing evidence before some tenth-century Spanish miniatures depicting bowed instruments, the bows being held in the middle or near one end. The theory of bowed strings was applied in the organistrum or hurdy-gurdy described by Odo of Cluny in the tenth century; a rosined wooden wheel turned with a handle setting all the strings in vibration at once. The Welsh crwth, believed to have been one of the earliest bowed instruments, may actually have been used as a plucked instrument during the first few centuries of its existence: there is no direct evidence that bowing occurred in Wales as early as it did in Spain.

From the early vielle, rebec and crwth to the modern violin family there has been steady development in power and variety of tone, and in technical facility. The mediaeval stringed instruments gradually assumed features similar to the violin—they were made from many pieces of wood stuck together, to give extra resonance, they began to curve in at the waist to allow more bowing freedom; the neck and finger-board became separate from the wood of the body, and the angle of the peg-box was altered to give a greater tension on the strings. No clear, direct line of descent leads to the violin family, which like the viol family emerged in its almost perfect form early in the sixteenth century.

The Renaissance period (1500-1600) brought with it a deepening of harmonic sense in music; instruments capable of playing chords, such as the lute, harp and organ and the newly invented clavichord and harpsichord, became an important means of expression. Single voice instruments were made in varied sizes so that complete harmonic effects could be obtained, even bass flutes and small, high bassoons being produced. At the same time an increased loudness and fullness of tone was sought, which may explain the emergence of the violin family, an apparently new design of instrument with no clear ancestors, some time before 1530.

The viol, in its perfect form appeared at about the same time as the violin, but its sombre colouring appealed to the Renaissance taste and it was firmly established long before the violin was accepted. Jambe de Fer in his *Epitome Musical* (1556) describes viols as being played by 'people of taste', whereas the violin's main use was for 'dances, weddings and mummeries'. As early as 1618, however, Praetorius tells us in his

Syntagma Musicum that the violin family is so well known that he need not say anything about it.

The main differences between the viol and violin families were the number and tuning of the strings, the thickness of the wood, and the manner of bowing. Viols normally had six strings, tuned like the lute in fourths with a third between the middle pair, whereas the violin family had at first three and then four strings, tuned in fifths. Viols, unlike the violins, had movable gut frets like the lute, and their thinner, less tense strings, with the thin wood used throughout the body, gave a sweeter, huskier tone than the violin, and greater blending power, but less vitality and contrast. The violin has a highly arched belly, and shallower ribs than the viol; its neck is sturdier, and the belly and back slightly overhang the ribs. Violin shoulders meet the neck at right-angles, whereas the viol's shoulders slope, and the violin has f-shaped instead of c-shaped sound-holes.

The parent instrument of the viol family is the *viola da gamba*, derived from the vielle, and held, as the name indicates, between the knees (*gamba* means leg). From the bass viol, with strings D G c e a d', a family of three or four sizes was developed, all played in the same way; music with a distinctly instrumental flavour began to be written for the consort of viols, and several sixteenth- and seventeenth-century authors give instructions on matching a chest of viols. The bow grip in viol playing brings the arm and wrist weight below instead of above the bow as in the violin; this makes it easier to equalize the pressure on up and down strokes, but is another factor detracting from volume, contrast and the modern conception of phrasing.

The parent instrument of the violin family was not the bass instrument but the alto—*viola da braccio*—our present viola. Its ancestry is much disputed; the peg-box and strings tuned in fifths point to the rebec, but the vaulted belly is only found in the lyra da braccio, which more closely resembles the violin in shape. There is also a claim that the viola was brought into Europe ready-formed from the North-East; certainly from the first it was known in Germany as the Polish *geige* (fiddle).

The early violin family consisted of a treble tuned as the present-day viola, and a tenor and bass each a fifth lower. Not until late in the sixteenth century did a smaller instrument tuned a fifth above the viola appear, called a *rabel à violino*, *ribecchino* or *violino*. Monteverdi in his *Orfeo* (1607) asks for ten *viole da braccio*, which would include violins, as well as the *violino piccolo* tuned a fourth or third higher still.

Viola da braccio became shortened to *viola* or *bratsche*; *quint* was sometimes used in France. The name *violoncello*, today shortened to cello, had appeared by 1700. Up to the end of the seventeenth century it was tuned a tone lower than today: most instruments made after that time were a little smaller to allow for the higher pitch. Cellos with five strings were popular about 1700.

The true bass of the violin family, tuned in fifths

and called the *gross-quint-bass* or *contrabass*, was a coarse, little-used instrument. Mattheson, in 1713, described the playing of it as 'labour fit for a horse'. The *violone*, double bass of the viol family was almost invariably preferred for its clearer, purer tone (Bach uses it as the bass of his string family), and the modern double bass is more likely to have come from this than the bass violin. A coarsening of the body has increased the tone, the six strings have become four or five, tuned in fourths, and the frets have disappeared. The sloping shoulders are retained, and bowing in the underhand viol manner still persists on the continent.

The lowest note on the double bass to the highest normally used on the violin covers a compass of over seven octaves; within that compass can be produced a wide variety of shades of tone and of volume. The members of the violin family blend easily with each other and with other instruments, and the ear does not tire of string tone as it does of, say, the wind tone used in Strauss's Serenade for thirteen wind instruments. For this reason the strings have become the core of the modern symphony orchestra, and because of the variety of effects obtainable tthrough different bowings, positions, pizzicato and muting, a fairly substantial repertoire exists for string orchestra.

The string quartet consists of two violins, viola, and cello: originally there was a tenor violin, like a small cello, and the viola would take the alto part instead of a second violin. Unfortunately the tenor instrument died out before 1700, and the viola now plays the true tenor part. In spite of the gap in register between cello and viola, however, the string quartet remains the most homogeneous and satisfactorily balanced chamber ensemble, and is the medium for some of the greatest music ever written.

The violin itself has changed only a little since it emerged during the sixteenth century, some fifty years after the viola. Methods of playing have undergone considerable alteration, however, and accessories are still being changed and improved. A string orchestra of Corelli's time would look and sound different to even the least knowledgeable observer if placed beside a modern string orchestra. Corelli's contemporaries would prop their violins against the chest, below the collar-bone. Chin-rests were clearly not needed; they only gained popularity during the nineteenth century, and the modern shoulder-rest would probably have seemed clumsy as well as unnecessary to Corelli.

Cello spikes would be absent from Corelli's orchestra, and probably many of the cellists would hold the bow with the hand beneath instead of above the stick, as viol-players did. This had for so long been the accepted way of bowing instruments held downwards or between the knees, that it was some considerable time before the violin method of bowing was invariably applied to the cello, as contemporary paintings show. The bows themselves would look strange to us, tapering to a point and lacking the curve of the wood towards the hair which gives the modern bow its spring and flexibility. A rather flat bridge and a short

B

fingerboard are other visible differences, and without doubt there would be audible differences, too. Continuous vibrato lends a roundness and suavity to modern string tone, aided by longer, more tense strings (see Chapter 8) and the use of upper positions on the lower strings. Corelli avoided the G string altogether whenever possible, either because it sounded too nasty or was too difficult to play on, and had he desired to use very high positions, he would have run off the end of his short fingerboard.

These are a few of the changes which have taken place in string performance; most of them are definite improvements. The modern orchestral players are a good deal more comfortable than their seventeenth-century counterparts—for one thing, the violinists and violists now sit down in the orchestra instead of standing up—except that the modern violist has to cope with even more unwieldy dimensions of his instrument.

In return for these standards of comfort and high quality of equipment, the modern string orchestral player is expected to contribute a technical dexterity which would have been considered of virtuoso standard one hundred and fifty years ago, and impossible two hundred and fifty years ago. Some modern orchestral scores could only be performed with complete accuracy by an orchestra of virtuosi—scores as early as Wagner's are so difficult that many string players produce only a rough approximation, or a judicious selection, of the notes. The lower instruments today share these technical demands; the times are past when a very simple, unimportant line, or no line at all, was written for the viola, because violists could not manage anything more difficult, and when the double basses merely doubled the cellos, simplifying the difficult passages. Bach and Handel used the orchestral viola with a definite awareness of their individual colouring but without requiring any extension of technique beyond the low positions. With Haydn and Mozart came a gradual extension into the higher register, and more and more technical attributes of the violins were expected from the orchestral violas during the nineteenth century, until Strauss and Debussy were using the section with no more technical restriction than the violins. The double bass could never aspire to such pyrotechnics as the smaller instruments, but it too has progressed in the upward extension of its register and the addition of such effects as muted basses and bass harmonics to the range of orchestral colours.

The orchestra is only one field in which these changes have taken place. In chamber music, viola technique extended more rapidly: before the close of the eighteenth century its status was equal to that of the second violin of the string quartet, and in solo music such as Mozart's Sinfonia Concertante very high positions and considerable technical problems are already encountered. The popularity of the small double bass as a solo instrument during the life-time of its greatest exponent, Dragonetti (1763-1846) gave it a new independence in certain chamber works, and must have awakened interest in the instrument's orchestral potentialities, judging from the difficult and free bass line in Beethoven's later symphonies and the works of his successors.

The delay between the establishment of the violin as a solo instrument with a varied technique and that of the lower three instruments was partly due to the falling-off in interest in the lower parts during the eighteenth century, when some composers began to prefer a melodic line with simple accompaniment to the more contrapuntal style which reached its peak with Johann Sebastian Bach. Practical considerations, such as the difficulty of constructing a viola which was not either too weak to be effective or too large to handle, also had a retarding effect. The cello suffered at first from rivalry of the popular bass viol, and the prevalence of underhand bowing must have slowed the advance of true cello bowing technique. The solo possibilities of the cello's tenor register also could not be properly developed until Jean Louis Duport (1749-1819) solved the problem of fingering by using the thumb as well as all the fingers of the left hand in high positions.

Whether instrumental technique follows composers' demands or composers have been inspired by technical discoveries of great performers, is a debatable point; something of each seems to be true. The early development of string technique was mainly accomplished by the great violinist-composers, so the question does not arise, but gradually specialization has become the rule, and we hear of modern composers approaching great performers for advice on the technical limits of their instruments. Today a violinist may be soloist, orchestral player or leader, or chamber music player: before 1800 he was likely to combine the roles of soloist and chamber instrumentalist with those of composer, orchestral leader-conductor (the leader or continuo-player, or both, conducted the orchestra) and teacher of violin and composition. The prodigious number of works produced by these performer-composers (four hundred concertos of Vivaldi, a hundred sonatas and a hundred and twenty-five solo concertos by Tartini, over two hundred string quartets and quintets by Boccherini) seem to indicate that specialization and creative productivity work in inverse ratio.

In the following chapters the technical progress of each instrument in turn will be traced, taking first the viola, which is the true parent-instrument of the family, emerging some fifty years before the violin.

II. THE VIOLA

The viola has perhaps a more varied history than any other instrument of the orchestra. From its original position as prima donna of the *braccio* family, it sank to second place with the advent of the violin, gradually taking over the part of the dying tenor violin and becoming a vague, filling-in nonentity with the increasing popularity of the trio sonata and keyboard continuo. Gaining, of necessity, an increased importance and technique during the eighteenth century with the emergence of the string quartet, it was not until the nineteenth century that the viola's individual tone colour and orchestral possibilities were recognized, and only in the present century has it gained any status as a solo instrument.

One reason for its rapid decline of popularity during the late sixteenth century was that the tone of the viola was far inferior to that of the violin, owing to its small dimensions in relation to its low pitch. In the cello, the low pitch is compensated by the extra deep ribs, but this is clearly impracticable in an instrument held beneath the chin. Another factor was the greater contrapuntal homogeneity of two instruments of the same pitch, which led the Italians to use two violins rather than violin and viola in the trio sonata. Later, the French and Germans were to prefer the contrast given by an instrument of lower pitch, thus leading towards the dissolution of the trio sonata, but until 1750 the only important part played by the viola was in the work of the contrapuntal composers, who treated each strand equally. Corelli, who used no viola in the *concertino* (solo group) of his concerti grossi, had to insert a *ripieno* (orchestral group) entry into the fugal expositions of the concertino. This would appear to give an unbalanced exposition, but as the concertino were generally professionals and the ripieno amateurs, probably the tone of several ripieno violists with their weak instruments would approximately balance the other entries. After this entry, the viola would resume its normal filling-in role.

Geminiani added a viola to the *concertino*, making a complete string quartet and giving the viola considerable importance as a contrapuntal line. Both Bach and Handel were conscious of the viola section's effectiveness as an individual colour within the string orchestra. Handel introduces divisi violas for a moment of special tension in his operas and choral works (see *Sieh'dort die blässe Schar*—Behold, a ghastly band—from *Alexander's Feast*) and Bach's sixth Brandenburg Concerto uses violas as the concertino section. They used only the lower positions however, which gave the instrument a very limited range, and wrote no solo music for it. Because of the paucity of its repertoire, no part at all in the trio sonata and little solo music to compensate, the viola was neglected by the better musicians, who preferred the violin. The only reason given for working hard on the viola was as a stepping-stone to the violin, and as few could play the instrument the composers would not risk writing difficult parts for it. A vicious circle was thus set up which took the best part of a century to be eliminated.

Quantz, writing about the viola in his *Versuch* (1752), finds it necessary to warn the violist against spoiling a passage played in unison with the violins. He points out that:

'One commonly regards the viola as something of little importance in music. The reason may perhaps be that it is often played by people who are still beginners in music or who have no special talent to distinguish themselves on the violin; or also because this instrument brings all too little advantage to its player. For this latter reason skilled people do not like to play it. I believe, nevertheless, that a violist must be just as skilled as a second violinist, to prevent the whole accompaniment from being defective.'

In the early eighteenth-century symphony, the doubling of the bass part an octave higher by the violas was a standard procedure most frequently varied by the insertion of a harmony note missing from the other parts; this method of using the unreliable instrument may be seen in the symphonies of J. W. A. Stamitz and his contemporaries. Karl Stamitz was bolder in using the viola, particularly in his chamber music, but a typical viola part in chamber music of the early eighteenth century has an occasional canonic entry, sustains chords and accompanying figures, doubles the bass in octaves or the treble in thirds.

The viola's most rapid emancipation came with the string quartet. Tartini (1692-1770) wrote many 'sonate a quattro', with no continuo, but they resemble the sinfonia, with its still bass line and negligible viola part, rather than the string quartet. Sammartini approached more closely to a chamber style with his quartets; they have a freer bass line and more rests, but no real improvement of the viola part was apparent until Haydn's opus 2. The third quartet of this set shows a great step forward for the viola, which takes its turn in the second minuet to predominate for one variation, holding a dolce melody accompanied by the other three instruments. (Possibly the viola was intended to be doubled on the horn, as wind parts have been discovered for some of these early quartets.) From then on, the importance of the viola part in Haydn's quartets increases until it is equal to the other two lower instruments, but the first violin always retains a certain predominance, and only the lower viola positions are used. In his symphonies, Haydn clearly mistrusts the viola section. The opening of number 104 in D major (The London) shows a viola line doubled by the bassoons most of the time, even when no other wood-wind are playing. The violas are never given an important entry after a rest, presumably they might forget to play it! There certainly seems to be evidence in support of Forsyth's statement that only those who were 'too wicked or too senile to play the violin' played the viola at that time.

Boccherini (1743-1808), who raised the status of the

cello in chamber music, did little for the viola except that in his opus 9 (1761) he used it to replace the second violin of the trio sonata; writing for the string trio thus formed on a homophonic instead of a contrapuntal basis, and passing arpeggios between the three instruments. The last quartets of Haydn and Mozart give all four parts of the string quartet an equal voice in the discussion, and in the quintets the first viola rivals the first violin in importance, but its technique is still limited. Difficult passages such as the triplet arpeggios in K.428 are kept mainly in the first position, and the viola line in the symphonies approximates more nearly to that of the cellos than the fiddles. Orchestral equality is only achieved in the contrapuntal development sections.

Mozart, like Haydn and Schubert, played the viola, and his understanding of its capabilities in the hands of a good player is apparent from the effective solo viola part of the Sinfonia Concertante, in which the violist was intended to tune his instrument up a semitone for extra brilliance. The viola performs the same technical feats as the violin, and today the violin tone often suffers by contrast with the viola's greater dimensions. The orchestral viola parts of this work (1779) are also amongst the most interesting of the century; used divisi, they sometimes support the solo viola unaccompanied. Divisi violas appear in several of Mozart's symphonies, after the Salzburg tradition; the most notable instance being the opening of the G minor Symphony K.550.

Beethoven's early quartets give the viola less scope than Mozart's chamber music, but he uses the solo tone colour fairly frequently in his late quartets, generally for short passages, as in the second movement of opus 131. In his symphonies, the viola is linked mainly with the cello line, but is gradually beginning to break away. An unsupported viola melody is still unknown (an 'exception to prove the rule' occurring in bar 267 of the Fourth Piano Concerto, where divisi violas bring back the rondo theme in disguise) but melodic unisons with the cellos appear in the andante of the Fifth Symphony and elsewhere. Contemporarily with Beethoven, Weber was trying to raise the standard of viola playing by writing technically difficult parts for it such as the viola obbligato in *Der Freischütz*, Act III, and he appears to have been one of the first orchestral composers to recognize the individuality of viola tone colour. Mendelssohn (himself a violist) tentatively experimented with the instrument, giving it an occasional expressive melody in his chamber music, but like Schubert he generally preferred to exploit its blending power and effectiveness in accompanying figuration.

The viola's emotional capabilities were fully grasped by Schumann, whose chamber music uses its high register (written, for the first time, with a treble clef) and gives it several attractive melodies. Unfortunately, in the Piano Quartet and Quintet, these are generally doubled on the piano. Several pieces for viola and piano, the *Märchenbilder*, and some for viola, clarinet and piano indicate Schumann's interest in the instrument, and in his Second Symphony the viola is at last completely independent of the other parts. Effective instances are the running quaver accompaniment to the wood-wind in Trio II, and the high repeated semiquaver chords, 'divisi a 3', in the coda of the same movement.

Many instruments beside the violin were influenced by Paganini's virtuoso technique, and the viola gained the first technically brilliant work of its repertoire through his direct request. Berlioz wrote *Harold in Italy* with a solo viola part for Paganini to play on his Stradivarius viola, although the violinist never actually performed it. A solo viola had been used with the orchestra before—in Mozart's Sinfonia Concertante, a suite by Telemann, a concerto by Stamitz, and one by Dittersdorf for viola and double bass, for instance—but *Harold*, with its contrasted use of low and high registers, double stops and rapid runs, was a new venture. Forsyth asserts that 'One hearing of *Harold in Italy* is quite enough to put the listener off the viola for the rest of his life', but the work is still played and enjoyed today, and it represents an important stage in the development of viola technique. Wagner was conscious of the viola's orchestral possibilities; he used it as a soprano, tenor or bass line, but very few orchestral violists even at the time of his later works were capable of playing the parts he wrote. Combinations of divided violas and cellos, broken chord effects and viola solos such as that in *Tristan* require very capable violists and give a highly individual colouring to his string writing.

Brahms usually keeps the orchestral violas in the lower positions: his string writing is often low and thick, but in his chamber music (particularly the quintets) he elevates the viola to a position of far greater importance than the second violin, which is apt to have a rather dull time playing in its weakest register. The third movement of opus 67, with an unmuted viola singing above three muted instruments, is a real opportunity for the violist, and the two songs with viola obbligato, besides his own arrangement of the clarinet sonatas, show Brahms's fondness for the instrument.

The French school used the viola less for its emotional effect, like the Germans and Tchaikovsky (in the romantic melody in *Romeo and Juliet*, for instance), than as a subtle tone colour. Both Debussy and Ravel exploit a certain nasal, almost wood-wind quality with great effect in their orchestral works and the quartets, particularly the third movement of Ravel's Quartet. Harmonics, pizzicato and sul ponticello effects are proved to sound particularly well on the viola, and modern composers have followed Richard Strauss in exploring other possibilities of the orchestral section. *Don Quixote* is notable for its high viola obbligato and a passage where the violas are divided into twelve parts: Stravinsky's *Le Sacre du Printemps* uses a glissando in harmonics on the violas, and a passage for six solo violas accompanied by cello pizzicato and harmonics. False harmonics (in Schoenberg's *Serenade*), varied pizzicato, close to and away from the bridge (in Berg's Violin Concerto), are the kind of thing the orchestral violist may expect to meet today, and the leader's solo capabilities are exploited quite frequently in the works of Vaughan Williams, Strauss, Bloch, Honegger, Mahler and other modern composers.

The twentieth century has seen the firm establishment of the viola as a solo instrument; with a technique almost as varied as the violin, in spite of the impediment to high position work given by the viola's wide shoulders. In this country, Lionel Tertis was primarily responsible for the recognition of the viola's solo capabilities, and his book *Cinderella No More* tells of a life-time successfully devoted to the propagation of the viola's gospel. The Tertis model viola, designed in collaboration with the violin-maker Arthur Richardson, was conceived from the practical viewpoint of obtaining the maximum sonority with the minimum difficulty of manipulation, a length of 16¾ inches being decided on.

The lead given by Mr. Tertis in this country, by the composer Hindemith (himself a viola player) in Germany, and by William Primrose in America, has aroused considerable interest in the medium on the part of modern composers. The Viola Concerto of Walton is already a standard item of concert repertoire (Walton's interest in the viola is borne out by his String Quartet); Bartók's Concerto, incomplete when he died, has been made ready for performance by Tibor Serly; and Fricker, Rivier and Rubbra are among those who have contributed to modern viola concertos. The special problems of balance in writing a viola concerto are overcome in various ways, by contrasting the pitch or style of writing in the solo and accompaniment, by reducing the string parts while the soloist is playing, or by accompanying the viola tone with wind instruments and reserving the strings mainly for the tuttis. Elgar sanctioned a viola arrangement of his Cello Concerto, which uses similar ways of rendering the soloist clearly audible and able to compete musically with the orchestra.

Sonatas and suites have also been written for viola and piano by twentieth-century composers: Bax, Benjamin, Bliss, Bloch, York Bowen, Britten, Hindemith, Reger and Vaughan Williams have contributed to what is becoming a fairly substantial recital repertoire, filled out by some good transcriptions of works for obsolete instruments, such as the Bach sonatas for gamba and the Schubert sonata for arpeggione. A glance at the Bloch Suite or the Stravinsky Elegy for viola reveals that all the violinist's technical attributes—double to quadruple stopping, varied harmonics, etc.—are required of the modern solo violist. Few people begin their musical studies on the viola, and it is in many ways more advisable to cope first with the smaller dimensions and wider repertoire of the violin. No longer, however, can the violin failures hope to get by on the viola; the music being written today requires the highest technical standards from all string players.

III. THE VIOLIN

The early history of violin technique lies mainly in the works of the great violinist-composers. The first to establish a basis of violin repertoire was Arcangelo Corelli (1653-1713), who holds a position of considerable importance in musical history as the earliest notable composer for the violin. Because of this, people tend to make other claims on his behalf, mainly untrue: that he was the first great violinist, that he extended the very elementary violin technique of his time, that he was the first to write violin sonatas containing contrasted movements, and other false assertions. These arise from a lack of knowledge about his predecessors. Long before Corelli was born, English composers at the court of James I were writing for violins in consort and with keyboard instruments, and German string playing was probably even in advance of the Italian technique during Corelli's lifetime. All Corelli's works are for the violin family, however, while his English contemporary Purcell wrote frequently for viols, and the German violin compositions of the period (with a few exceptions) are more noted for their technical interest than their musical value.

A modest, amiable man, Corelli was no great innovator; what he did was to accept the already quite considerable heritage of Italian violin writing, and by his good taste and creative ability consolidate its best aspects, eradicating the crudeness which makes the early works less acceptable to our ears. His fame as a violinist was considerable, but his teachers Benvenuti and Bragnoli had great fame before him, and there were fine violinists in the generation before that. The technique of his compositions is indeed rather limited compared with certain earlier works; he aimed at purity and elegance rather than any exploration into technical brilliance, and is said to have been astounded by the technical achievements of the German violinist Strungk who visited his country. Corelli does not go above the third position, and his double stops are fairly straightforward, generally used when the two voices of a fugal exposition must be played on one instrument in the solo sonatas.

Carlo Farina, writing before Corelli was born, used pizzicato, double stops and rapid passages, even col legno, to little musical account, but with anticipation of later techniques. Marini used tremolo in 1617, and the famous score of Monteverdi's *Combattimento* (1624) shows tremolos and pizzicati for orchestral strings. In 1626 Marini revealed a considerable double stopping technique in his opus 8 *Capriccio che due violini sonano quattro parti*; he also used triple stops, and his trills point to the use of third position. The Germans were writing up to the sixth and even seventh positions before Corelli began to compose, and both Germans and Italians had experimented with complicated double stops and chords, using scordatura (the re-tuning of one or more strings to facilitate certain stops, either

c

for a passage or a whole movement). Schmelzer in 1664 used the violin as a transposing instrument, and his pupil Biber wrote twelve sonatas (*c.* 1670) with a different tuning for each.

The grouping of contrasted movements to form sonatas was a firmly established custom among the Italians by the time Corelli produced his opus 1. Two basic types, the *sonata da chiesa*, made up of abstract movements, and the *sonata da camera*, with dance titles to its movements, had grown up; by Corelli's time a move towards the reconciliation of the two types was becoming apparent. Fontana, Uccellini and Legrenzi had followed the lead given by Rossi and Marini in establishing a set pattern of movements; a dignified slow opening usually in 4-4 time, a quick fugal second movement in the church sonata and a gigue or corrente in the chamber type, a short slow third movement, generally in 3-2 time and occasionally in a different key from the others, more smoothly harmonic in effect, and a lively final movement.

Corelli's opp. 1-5 are all built on this scheme, although he occasionally varies the order of the movements, or interpolates *moto perpetuo* passages or movements of semiquavers for the violin; these now sound rather dull with their endless arpeggio figures over simple chords, but probably made a very brilliant effect at the time. Opus 1 (1683) and opus 3 (1689) are sets of twelve *sonate di chiesa* for two violins with organ continuo—the use of the organ becomes apparent in long pedal points while the violins play extended arpeggio passages. Several of the *chiesa* movements are clearly dances, although not given a title; Corelli always uses three contrapuntal parts in his church sonata dances, however, while those of the chamber sonatas may have only two. The chamber sonatas for two violins with clavier, opus 2 and opus 4 (1694) are made up of dances invariably in simple binary form after the traditional style; only the chaconne (as in opus 2, no. 12) breaks away from this pattern. The keys and harmonies of the sonatas are simple and consistent, particularly in the slow movements. Corelli obtains some lovely effects by means of suspensions, and to give some variety from the normal bustling violins over a staid bass, he sometimes introduces an energetic bass part in quavers while the violins sustain harmonies and suspensions.

In his opus 5, (c. 1700) a set of twelve sonatas, six in the church and six in the chamber style, for solo violin and continuo, Corelli naturally has less scope for counterpoint. In the church sonatas he attempts to retain the polyphonic element by the use of double stops, but he abandons contrapuntal treatment in the last six sonatas. The first movement of sonata no. 1 contains very rapid changes of mood, and an extra movement with violin semiquavers throughout is interpolated after the free fugal movement; this happens in most of the solo sonatas, which are more brilliant than Corelli's other works. Sonata no. 12 consists of a set of twenty-three variations on the theme *La Follia*; in it, Corelli goes to the limit of his technical resources to obtain variety, and shows a remarkable understanding of the effects obtainable on the violin by both left hand and bowing dexterity.

Corelli's last published works were the set of twelve concerti grossi opus 6, *c.* 1712. The earliest published works in this form were those of Gregori (1698), Torelli (1709) and Valentini (1710), but Muffat reports hearing Corelli conduct his own concerti grossi as early as 1682, so in this case he may have been an innovator. Certainly it was he who firmly established the form, using the concertino of two violins and cello in alternation with the orchestra to gain dynamic contrast. The first eight are in the church style, and probably composed for church occasions; the last four are chamber concertos and contain a free treatment of the solo group. The individual instruments are allowed to step forward, particularly in no. 12 where the first violin dominates as a virtuoso solo. This work was to point the way for many composers, including Vivaldi and Handel.

The noticeably small range in pitch of Corelli's violin writing was partly due to the limitations of the contemporary instrument, and the way of holding it. The violin neck was shorter, broader and more round than it is today, and projected straight out in the same plane as the body. The bridge was probably flatter and about one-twelfth of an inch lower than today, although it would vary from instrument to instrument until Stradivarius's pattern or a close variant came to be generally used. The fingerboard narrowed towards the bridge end, and was considerably (about two and a half inches) shorter than today, allowing seven positions at the most. Gut strings, no chin-rest, and a shorter, slighter bass bar were the other main structural differences: G strings wound with silver did not appear until later in the eighteenth century (they are mentioned by Quantz in 1752, Löhlein in 1774). The convex bow with rather slacker hair than today used on a gut G string probably did not produce a very pleasant tone; Corelli avoids the G string whenever possible.

Another reason for confining his writing to the first three positions on the three upper strings must have been the awkwardness of shifting, and of bowing on the G string at all, when the violin was held propped against the collar-bone or the breast. By the middle of the eighteenth century this habit had given way to that of holding the violin on the shoulder, with the chin to the right of or over the tailpiece, and L'Abbé le fils (J. B. Saint-Sévin, 1761) advocated the modern method with the chin on the left. The chin-rest did not appear until the following century (Spohr claimed to have invented it *c.* 1820). Modern use of rigid or sprung shoulder-rests gives the instrument a stability that was entirely lacking in the eighteenth century; this is probably why some of the fingerings in Geminiani's violin method, for instance, seem peculiarly intricate, although the basic left hand position he indicated is the same as today.

Francesco Geminiani (*c.* 1674-1762) was a pupil of Corelli and possibly also of Alessandro Scarlatti. Failing to please as conductor of the orchestra at Naples, on account of his 'wild and erratic' beat, he went to England and there established a considerable reputation as violinist, composer and teacher. His technique was bolder than that of Corelli, and few English violinists could play his opus 1 (twelve solo sonatas, 1716). Perhaps this is why they criticized the sonatas as lacking proportion and refinement compared with Corelli's works. To our ears they sound both refined and interesting; their melodies have a pleasant chromaticism and the modulations are often unusual. Always interested in extending the boundaries of instrumental music, Geminiani added a viola to the concertino unit of the concerto grosso, giving more scope for polyphonic development, and experimented with rare chords such as the Neapolitan sixth and augmented sixths. His theoretical works, a guide to harmony, the *Art of Playing on the Violin* (1751) and *A Treatise on Good Taste* (1749), throw interesting light on musical practice of the period.

Geminiani's violin method was the first to be published in England, and it preceded that of Leopold Mozart by five years. Some of its instructions are surprisingly modern, others were old-fashioned even then. Great emphasis is laid on expressiveness, music must, he says, 'express Sentiments, strike the Imagination, affect the Mind, and command the Passions'. The swell within a long note is pointed out as one of the violin's chief beauties, and continuous vibrato is recommended, (as opposed to the German flute's ornamental vib-

rato). A useful section on ornaments and their performance shows the prevalent Italian ideas of the time;
a long appoggiatura, for instance, conveyed 'Love
Affection, Pleasure, etc.'

Technically, the examples, instructions and 'twelve
pieces in different stiles' cover most of the important
left hand work except for consecutive trills and double
trills, but the bowing exercises are far less complete
than those of Leopold Mozart. Seven positions are
demonstrated on all four strings, although the musical
examples do not use them. Geminiani's suggestion of
marking the beginner's fingerboard in tones and semitones may hark back to the viol frets, and both his bow
grip and method of holding the violin against the
chest, below the collar-bone, were out-dated, according to Mozart (who advocates gripping with the
chin to the *right* of the tail-piece), but his method of
gaining a good left hand position by placing one finger
on each string was adopted in Mozart's second
edition.

Antonio Vivaldi (1680-1743), less of a theorist than
Geminiani, held a position of far greater influence
through his extension of the concerto form, raising the
Italian concertos to such a state of perfection that his
works were models for many years. The number of his
concertos is estimated at over four hundred, besides
the less individual trio sonatas, thirty-nine operas, an
oratorio and various lesser works. All these were
written in between his frequent travels as a violin
virtuoso and his work as leader of the orchestra at St.

Mark's Venice, and director of music at the Ospidale della Pietà.

The Ospidale was a home for orphan girls, and the standard of orchestral playing there was amazingly high. Commissioned to write two concertos a month for them, Vivaldi was free to experiment with different tone colours, varied wind and string solos, and a ripieno given individuality by the use of wind. In the concerto grosso he expanded the concertino to four violins, and reduced it to two, disrupting it to allow individual solos, but retaining formal unity by developing his episodes out of previous material.

Vivaldi's concertos show the influence of the opera, where virtuosity was given more scope, as well as of the earlier concerto composers, Corelli, Torelli, Albinoni and others. His technique as a violinist must have been considerable, for although the double and triple stopping passages make frequent use of open strings or scordatura, he writes runs up to the eighth position, and is reported by a contemporary violinist to have played far higher himself. His compositions lie well under the hand—a violinist's string compositions are always easier to play and generally more brilliant in effect than those of a non-violinist—and his combinations of varied bow techniques with arpeggio figurations were unprecedented in their brilliance. The bariolage, in which an open string continues like a pedal through a series of arpeggiated chords, was a device taken from Marini and Scarlatti, given a new effectiveness by Vivaldi's advanced bow technique and higher positions, and inherited by Bach in his concertos and the E major solo partita.

Bowings used by Vivaldi include various types of staccato, with as many as twenty-four staccato notes beneath a single slur. His slow movements leave ample room for free embellishment on the part of the soloist, and he expanded the cadenza at the end of the first allegro to new, brilliant proportions. On the G string he uses rapid bowings, and several positions, but never a slow sustained melody: his orchestral string writing is colourful (and often programmatic; there are concertos called *The Tempest*, *Repose*, etc.) and uses effects such as pizzicato, tremolo and muted strings. Locatelli and Tartini were to write more brilliant music for solo violin, but Vivaldi established the broad, sonorous type of playing expected by Bach in his violin works; and in his concertos Vivaldi establishes his right to a position amongst the famous experimenters in orchestration.

Locatelli's concertos and sonatas are musically interesting: he was a pupil of Corelli and settled in Amsterdam as violin virtuoso and teacher, but his caprices and studies can give no clear information as to the state of contemporary violin technique, as they are clearly experimental and often ugly. His attempts to explore the utmost limitations of the violin's capabilities, however, had an effect in the following century when they inspired Paganini to further interest in the violin.

The dominating figure of the following years is that

of Giuseppe Tartini (1692-1770), who is reputed to have discovered the resultant tone, inaugurated the use of thicker, tauter strings, and made several improvements to the bow, correcting its outward bulge, diminishing the head, and using lighter wood fluted at the heel for a surer grip. His considerable reputation as soloist and teacher led to the foundation in 1728 of the violin school which was to earn the title *School of the Nations*. His one hundred and twenty-five concertos advanced both violin and cello technique considerably, particularly with regard to bowing; his variations on a theme of Corelli make an interesting study in bowing today, and his letter to Signora Maddalena Lombardini gives some useful instructions in violin technique.

Scraps of verse and minor lyrics are attached to the concertos, for Tartini was a religious romantic; typical of his character is the Devil's Trill Sonata, supposed to have been played to him in a dream by the Devil. Technically very difficult, this sonata (one of a hundred solo sonatas, as opposed to one published trio sonata) contains consecutive single and double trills, as well as a free use of high positions and treble stops, which show Tartini's technical capabilities. Through J. C. Bach, Tartini influenced Mozart's concerto form: the last of the great composer-violinists, his successors were to be found more in the German than the Italian school of the next century.

The German violin school, after the very rapid technical development demonstrated by the virtuosi Baltzar, Biber, Walther and others during the seventeenth century, concentrated more on the performance of polyphonic music on a single instrument than on the extension of the upper range or varied bow techniques. Italian influence, which permeated Europe, was imported through Pisendel, who studied with Vivaldi and wrote unaccompanied sonatas for violin as well as the usual concertos and sonatas. The difficulty of the triple and quadruple stopping in Bach's unaccompanied compositions is not carried into the accompanied writing, and his use of seventh position for the orchestral violins in the B Minor Mass is exceptional. Haydn and Mozart were freer in their use of high positions, particularly in the quartets and Mozart's serenades, but Spohr (1784-1859) was the violinist who restored the Germans to a position of importance in the realm of violin virtuosity, and he was of the French school of performance.

After the death of Tartini, leadership in virtuosity passed for a time to France, although the French school was originated by an Italian living in Paris—Viotti. France was the last European country to renounce the viol and accept the prevalent Italian forms and advanced violin technique, but Leclair (1697-1764) shows in his sonatas that by 1750 the French were at least as advanced technically in violin playing as the other countries. Certain technical developments occurred first of all in France during the eighteenth century, such as the application of harmonics to the violin (Mondonville, 1738), thumb positions to the cello

(Duport, 1770) and, above all, the perfection of the bow by Tourte (1747-1835).

It is not surprising, therefore, that the French violin school should take the lead. Viotti (1755-1824), the son of a blacksmith who played the horn, settled in Paris after touring Switzerland, Germany and Russia as virtuoso violinist. In a direct line of pupils (through Somis and Pugnani) from Corelli, he had by 1783 established himself as the greatest violinist in France, and he moved in a circle of eminent musicians, living with his friend Cherubini. A favourite at court, he became manager of the Theâtre de Monsieur, and remained there, in spite of the revolutionary stirrings, until the eve of the arrest of the royal family, when he left for England. Here he broke his resolution (of several years' standing) not to play in public, and performed at nearly all the Salomon concerts of 1794-5, with great success. Wrongly suspected of revolutionary tendencies, he was forced to flee from England, but returned in 1801 to found an unsuccessful business as a wine-merchant. His health and fortunes steadily declined until his death, but he left behind him a considerable number of works, and a reputation of being the founder of modern violin technique.

His compositions are the first to bridge the gap between the eighteenth- and nineteenth-century conceptions of violin playing. Carefully constructed and written with a thorough knowledge of the instrument, even occasionally containing an original idea, his twenty-nine concertos and many smaller works make pleasant listening for a time, but spell boredom for the pianist or orchestra. As the technical requirements make a useful preparation for the romantic concertos, the twenty-second concerto (in A minor) is still used for teaching purposes.

Among Viotti's famous pupils was Pierre Rode, another virtuoso whose concertos are overweighted with reiterated crotchets in the orchestral parts and have therefore been relegated to teaching material. Rode's attempt to add warmth and drama to Viotti's style of composition merely emphasises the fact that all the expression is confined to the solo violin, the accompaniment becoming not so much a passenger as a hindrance. His only works in regular use today, the twenty-four caprices covering a variety of advanced technical problems, have no accompaniment. Rode was a professor at the Paris Conservatoire, and with Baillot and Kreutzer wrote for it a famous violin method. These violinists were also leading virtuosi of their time, but their many amiable concertos are forgotten even by teachers, and Kreutzer's forty-two studies are the only reasons for recalling him, apart from the Kreutzer Sonata of Beethoven.

Although we rarely hear the compositions of Viotti and his contemporary virtuosi at concerts today, however, it is as well to remember that we are partly indebted to them for the brilliant style of violin writing in Beethoven's Violin Concerto.

Niccolò Paganini (1782-1840) was next to gain an unprecedented celebrity in the realm of violin virtuosity, but quite apart from this development of fiery technique, his contemporary Ludwig Spohr (1784-1859) was gaining a reputation as a virtuoso in the line of the French school. Spohr worked as a boy for ten hours a day, learning from Franz Eck and imitating his greatly admired model Rode. His wide vibrato and singing tone, with heavy bowing even in quick passages, were the exact antithesis of Paganini's brittle brilliance, but his left hand technique was masterly in both double stops and stretches. Although unpretentious, his playing was widely acclaimed, and his works—including operas, oratorios, nine symphonies, many chamber works and fifteen concertos—were well received. His violin school (1831, as late as this the chin-rest was regarded as unnecessary) gained wide currency. Fond of experimenting with different combinations of instruments as in the double quartets, symphony for two orchestras, and quartet-concertos, he tended to make his works top-heavy by favouring the first or solo violin, and only occasional performances are heard today outside Germany.

Paganini is another composer whose originality is obscured by an excess—this time of technical display. Having gained, through talent, youthful drudgery enforced by his father, and an extreme natural flexibility of the hands, a technical ability never even approached by any previous violinist, he had to produce works difficult enough to show off his capabilities. Consequently, a certain natural talent for composition, backed by a training in harmony and counterpoint

from a pupil of Paer, was wasted on a series of display
pieces which roused the audiences of Europe to a frenzy
of appreciation when performed by their composer, but
which have little musical value.

Paganini, after breaking away from his over-strict
father, led a life of incredible successes on the concert
platform mingled with love affairs, gambling losses and
increasing illness. Innumerable legends have grown up
around him, so that it is difficult to separate the truth
from the legend; certainly, however, he was Director
of Music to Napoleon's sister, who also made him Cap-
tain of the Royal Bodyguard. A period (1801-4) during which he did not perform aroused rumours of
imprisonment; actually he was living with a lady of
rank in Tuscany, and his interest was temporarily absorbed by the guitar, for which he produced several
compositions.

The discovery of Locatelli's caprices brought him a
renewed interest in the violin, and his performances
in Italy and abroad (for fees such as £5,000 for twelve
nights in England) never failed to create a furore until
disease caused his retirement and rapid death. His
astounding technique was gained in his youth, and when
famous he never practised between concerts. Most of
the actual technical effects he used had been discovered
earlier; he is invariably accredited, for instance, with
the discovery of left hand pizzicato, which had been
used by Walther as early as 1688. Mestrino had used
the chromatic glissando before 1790, and Paganini's
fingering of the chromatic scale actually appears first

in Geminiani's violin tutor, 1756. False and double harmonics, however, had not been used before, and it was the way in which he used these tricks that made his playing remarkable. By contrasting extremes of pitch (harmonics and G string passages) using each string as a different tone colour with a range of three octaves, combined pizzicato and arco runs, guitar effects, passages in thirds, sixths, octaves and tenths, and innumerable varieties of spiccato bowing, he could make the violin sound like several different instruments—like a whole orchestra, according to contemporary reports.

Paganini's twenty-four caprices and two concertos are quite frequently played today but never, perhaps, with that bewitching brilliance which caused superstitious contemporaries to believe him a devil. Schumann, Liszt, Brahms and Rachmaninoff have paid lasting tribute to the violinist by founding works on his caprices; his own compositions hold the repertory more for their charm and brilliance than for any deep musical content.

Little has been added to the range of technical effects obtainable on the violin since the time of Paganini. Progress has been apparent more in the application of his effects to the lower instruments, and to the chamber music and orchestral music of the present century. Since the time of Berlioz, the string section of the orchestra has gradually acquired a range of technical effects far exceeding the variety obtainable on any other section.

I. LEOPOLD AND W. A. MOZART   *(artist unknown)*

L. Mozart holds the violin high on his shoulder, instead of propping it against the collar-bone in the earlier style depicted by Dou in his self-portrait (*overleaf*). The picture of Gow (*overleaf*) is the latest of the three, as by this time the bow has acquired a nose instead of a point, but the finger-board is still fairly short, and Gow holds the violin without a chin-rest and with his chin to the right of the tail-piece.

3. NIEL GOW 1727-1823

Henry Raeburn 1756-1823

2. GERARD DOU 1613-1675 *self-portrait*

Bowing may be varied—détaché, martelé, slurred, staccato, spiccato, and several other types of bowing are expected from the average orchestral player. Tonal variety from the instruction 'at the heel' or 'at the point', from repeated down or up bows, and from various combinations of divisi are effective with a large body of strings (see the Elgar *Serenade for Strings*, and orchestral scores of Delius); Strauss revealed the wealth of effect obtainable from divisi tremolo in *Don Quixote*.

Pizzicato orchestral effects have been extended since Paganini's time, as they are more effective in ensemble playing than solo. Simultaneous bowing and left hand pizzicato, arpeggiated and banjo-fashion pizzicato chords, pizzicato glissando, 'snap' pizzicato (letting the strings snap against the fingerboard) and pizzicato with the fingernail are all to be found in the scores of Bartók (particularly his Violin Concerto). Other effects include pizzicato harmonics, the 'slap' of the jazz band double bass player, who strikes the string with his palm, pizzicato with the thumb (used by Sibelius on the viola in *Pelleas and Melisande*), tremolando pizzicato (used most effectively by Elgar to accompany the cadenza to his Violin Concerto), pizzicato doubling arco a common effect in the symphonies of Mahler) and pizzicato with exaggerated vibrato—a favourite direction of Stravinsky.

Varieties of tremolo apart from the normal bowed and fingered types are given by glissandi and harmonics played tremolo, by a bowed-fingered tremolo (on the violas in Dvořák's 'New World' Symphony), and by com-

D

binations of different types of tremolo and non-tremolo. Col legno (with the wood), sul tasto (over the finger-board) and sul ponticello (on the bridge) may be combined with tremoli or non-tremoli and glissandi, and many of these effects may be used simultaneously to produce new timbres. Mutes, apart from their normal use, may be used by only a part of the section, or they may be added (or removed) gradually, player by player, as in Ravel's *La Valse*.

The use of the tone colour of a single string, double and triple stops, all kinds of harmonics, multiple divisi, glissandi and portamenti, is now an accepted technique of string orchestration. Less common sounds are occasionally required to give a particular atmosphere, and we find such directions as 'bow below the bridge' (basses in Strauss's *Salome*), scordatura (mis-tuning of the strings) and 'wie eine Fidel' (like a country fiddler)—(both in Mahler's Fourth Symphony), quarter tones, and even 'tap with the bow on the back of the instrument' (of doubtful value to the instrument). Altogether, it seems that the string family entirely justifies its position as the basis of the modern symphony orchestra, for apart from having a tone of which the ear tires less quickly than any other family of instruments, it has an ever increasing wealth of combinations and effects with which to vary that tone.

The fact that orchestral players today must have all aspects of violin technique at their finger-tips reveals a further branch of progress during the past century—in the training of the professional violinist. There has always been a very small, select group of performers who are able to see a piece of music, imagine it in terms of violin tone and so co-ordinate their muscles (with practice) as to produce the pictured sounds. Those who carry this ability to the highest degree normally begin at an early age and may become our most eminent soloists. Progress in training is applied more to the slightly less gifted musicians, who may possess the musical vision but lack such spontaneous muscular application to the instrument, or may simply have taken up the instrument a little too late. Carl Flesch's analysis of technique in his *Art of Violin Playing* is perhaps the most authoritative general treatise for the guidance of teachers, but O. Ševčik's analytical method of tackling both left hand and bow technique by breaking down each large problem into a series of small exercises may be of the greatest practical value in making advanced technique possible for the less muscularly able player.

IV. THE CELLO

Originally tuned a tone lower than today, the cello soon assumed its present-day pitch and proportions, which gave it a tone superior to the viola, owing to the deep ribs. The five-stringed cello used by Bach for his sixth unaccompanied suite soon died out, but high positions (Jean Duport introduced thumb positions in 1770) have given it a range suitable for solo work. The solo repertoire is small, but varied in comparison with that of the viola, and the cello's position in chamber music has always been of the greatest importance.

Until 1625 the cello and viola da gamba were both used as the basis of the string family; after that date the cello gradually ousted its softer-toned rival, first in Italy and Germany, much later in France. The French *vingt-quatre violons*, however, almost certainly included cellos, not bass viols. A. Scarlatti and Purcell both used a four-part string orchestra with double basses doubling cellos at the octave, but in his chamber music, Purcell preferred to use the gamba and violone. Legrenzi's orchestra at St. Mark's, Venice, in 1685 used violins except for the bass line, but most of the orchestral music at the time specified neither family; any available instrument played the part. By 1756 the cello supremacy must have been firmly established for L. Mozart to say in his Violin School 'It is the most common instrument on which to play the bass'. C. P. E.

Bach also names the cello and harpsichord as the ideal continuo combination, although this was the realm in which the gamba took longest to die, the French having a liking for a gamba continuo, alone, highly ornamented, to give scope for their virtuosi.

The first sign that the cello was to develop its technique came with the solo cello sonatas of D. Gabrieli (c. 1659-1690): Ariosti and Bononcini also composed for the cello, but there were no cello compositions to rival Corelli's violin works until after 1750. Low positions only were used because the wide spacing of the notes made shifting difficult, and Bach's unaccompanied suites show that chords and double stops were far less frequent on the cello than the violin. The orchestral writing of Bach, Handel and their contemporaries shows a very limited cello line, almost invariably doubled by the bass or violone, the left hand of the continuo and sometimes the bassoon.

The fact that Bach's orchestral cellists at Leipzig were amateurs, University undergraduates, explains the simplicity of the orchestral cello line in comparison with the solo suites, or the first violin part (led by a professional). His scoring would also be affected by the availability of actual instruments—no official cello was at his disposal until 1729, the year of the St. Matthew Passion, and the last year in which he used the viola da gamba as an obbligato instrument. Four cantatas of 1731 have obbligati for cello (No. 56 giving the instrument a pictorial representation of the billowing sea), but Bach sometimes preferred to use the violoncello piccolo, an instrument smaller than the normal cello but larger than the tenor violin, with probably five strings, four tuned as the modern cello and one a fifth higher. The existence at this time of the viola pomposa, an extra large viola, and the viola da spalla, a small cello carried by itinerant musicians slung from the shoulder by a strap, has left some doubt as to the size and tuning of the instruments intended: the sixth cello suite of Bach, for instance, may have been intended for a small or a normal-sized cello with five strings.

Occasional thematic excursions of the cello alone are found in early eighteenth-century chamber music; Purcell and the Italians had already freed the cello from the continuo to this extent, and caused separate cello and continuo parts to be published.

The first cello instruction book appeared in 1741, written by Michel Corrette. Bowing methods at this time were, like those of the violin, largely a matter of choice; viol bowing was frequently used, and in proper cello bowing the thumb might be placed either on the hair or the stick, some distance from the nut. The middle of the bow only was recommended for use by Corrette, who followed the school of Bononcini. This early cello method discourages the use of the fourth finger in the higher positions—none of which go very high.

Cello music began to show an improving technique. Jacopo Bassevi Cervetto (1682-1783) wrote sonatas for the cello resembling those of Tartini for the violin, with scale passages, double stops, and even a rare excursion into the treble clef, as well as sonatas for three cellos, an alternative to the normal trio sonata instrumentation also used by de Fesch. Cello consciousness was increasing, and although solo cello sonatas were rare, the instrument was gradually freeing itself from the continuo of chamber works and taking an independent melodic line. Anton Filtz (1733-60) a German cellist actually names the cello first in his opus 6, sonatas for 'violoncello obbligato, flauto traverso e violino e basso'. The keyboard continuo began gradually to disappear from chamber music, a process revealed in the titles of works. *Con violoncello e basso continuo*, predominant in the 1750's, indicates that the continuo is essential; *col basso continuo ossia violoncello*, common in the 1760's, makes it optional while *e violoncello*, the usual formula of the 1770's rules out the continuo altogether.

In 1770 appeared Jean Louis Duport's *Essai sur le doigter du violoncelle et la conduite de l'archet, avec une suite d'exercices*. This work was to lay the foundations of modern cello technique, standardizing the bowing method and, above all, evolving a clear system of thumb positions which made available the highest cello register. The fingerboard, like that of the violin, had gradually to be lengthened to make room for the highest positions. A later development, the adjustable tailpin (a non-adjustable pin is depicted as early as 1618, in Praetorius's *Syntagma Musicum*) gave greater stability to the instrument and therefore ease of manipulation, apart from the added resonance of a wooden floor. It also gave those ladies who shunned the impropriety of a large instrument held between the knees a new opportunity to play it 'side-saddle'! Servais (1807-66) is said to have introduced the pin when old age and infirmity made it difficult for him to grip the cello between his knees, or rest it on a stool. It is now universally used, but it is surprising to find in an English book on the cello, printed in 1923, the words 'if the student makes use of a sliding pin, these instructions cannot be observed in every respect. . . .'

Orchestral cello parts, like those of the viola, suffered a certain deterioration with the symphonists of the early eighteenth century: from being an individual strand in a mainly contrapuntal texture, melodic and fully exploited as a tonal colour (see Bach's third Brandenburg Concerto, Handel's cello writing in *Alexander's Feast*) the cello line became a mere succession of bass notes to the harmony, doubled by the basses and sometimes the violas. Haydn and Mozart gradually raised the status of the orchestral cello again, but Boccherini in his opus 1 quartets (1761) really used his cello as a soloist in the ensemble, while giving the bass line to the second violin. The quintets of Boccherini, as befit the compositions of a great cellist, lift the instrument from obscurity to a dazzling predominance.

Haydn's early chamber works show that he still thinks of the cello as being doubled at the octave by the bass (see e.g., the first chord of opus 33, no. 3, last movement), but later the cello line gains in interest along with the second violin and viola. His orchestral cello parts are far less free, except for the cello solos in the symphonies, written for his fine leading cellist at Esterhazy; even when separated from the basses, as in the slow movement of the Military Symphony, they are still rather dull. The Cello Concerto, on the other hand, employs a wide technical range and is today considered difficult to play; some of the cello solos in the symphonies require a good technique. Mozart frees the cellos from the basses less frequently than Haydn, but his use in the piano trios is more thematic and interesting, and his quartets, particularly those for Frederick William II who was a cellist, give it an importance equal to the first violin. Solo parts such as the florid obbligato to 'Batti, batti' in *Don Giovanni* show that he understood the instrument's technical capabilities.

Beethoven freed the orchestral cello from the bass line, and wrote for it as the lighter, more melodic instrument it is. From the Eroica Symphony onwards this becomes increasingly apparent, until in the Choral Symphony they are not once written on the same stave. Haydn had taken his cello up to d', but Beethoven, in the solo from *Prometheus*, writes up to g', and he frequently uses the treble clef (writing, for some obscure reason, an octave higher) for high passages. This was long before the treble clef had been introduced for the viola. Beethoven's chamber music with piano gives the cello a part of real importance, and his five cello sonatas are an important addition to the repertoire. He pointed the way for the Romantic composers with pizzicato effects like those in opus 59, no. 1 (slow movement), and although his orchestral cello melodies are always doubled by viola, bassoon, or both, for him the cello was no longer just a bass instrument.

Schubert's cello writing is particularly warm and effective in his chamber music. He chooses two cellos for the C major Quintet, instead of the two violas of Mozart and Beethoven, and uses them independently and in unison with such effect that one is convinced while hearing it that this is the ideal chamber ensemble. The cello duet which introduces the second subject in the first movement, and the decorated return of the second movement melody, must be amongst the very finest pieces of cello writing. The piano trios and 'Trout' Quintet also contain important, difficult cello parts, and Schubert's melodic use of the orchestral cello is well in advance of Beethoven's, going freely into the tenor register. Weber's operas were also using the cello melodically at this time, sometimes divisi as in *Oberon*, and Rossini's divisi cello opening to the *William Tell* overture popularized this technique.

Mendelssohn took the cello a stage further in the orchestra with his melodic writing for it, and he was fond of low-lying harmonic figuration for divisi cellos, but his chamber music gives the cellist a very dull time. Berlioz and Wagner used each section of the strings effectively for its own individual colour, Wagner dividing his cellos freely, and Schumann gives the cello some interesting effects like the ponticello passage in the D minor Trio and scordatura in the Piano Quartet, but these composers did little to improve the technique of the instrument.

Schuman's Cello Concerto, although it contains some technical difficulties, gives no sense of display and is essentially lyrical. The Nationalist school, however, accepted the cello as an instrument capable of virtuoso display—Boccherini's writing had pointed to this even in the previous century—and the concertos of Dvořák, Lalo and Saint-Saëns all combine the display element successfully with lyrical cello writing. The Tchaikovsky Rococo Variations are very much a display piece: Brahms's Double Concerto and Elgar's Cello Concerto, on the other hand, although extremely technically difficult, never use virtuosity for its own sake.

Brahms left a record of his increasing interest in the cello by rewriting the B major Trio opus 8, giving the cello part new warmth and interest. In the string sextets the two cellos move mainly together, with some independence in the slow movement of the G major, but in his orchestral writing Brahms gives them independent and often expressive parts covering a wide range.

Later scores show that the cello was by this time firmly established not only as an individual melodic or bass instrument with a wide range and technique, but as one capable of unexpected tricks and effects, particularly pizzicato effects. The pizzicato glissando is very effective on the cello, as used by Bartók in his *Concerto for Orchestra*, and Bax gains a disturbing

effect with tremolo pizzicato in *Tintagel*. Debussy demands a wide variety of cello effects in *La Mer*, and a
'tremolo glissando' in *Rondes de Printemps*; Stravinsky
uses pizzicato harmonics in *Avant du Rossignol*. Schoenberg's *Verklärte Nacht* (1899) perhaps shows most
clearly the status of the cello in modern writing; technically and musically the two cellos are equal to the
two violas and violins, passage work and special effects
are freely interchanged.

An increasing number of technically brilliant cellists also ensures a steady increase in the solo repertoire. Cellist-composers are a rarer breed than violinist-
composers, but great cellists have had their influence
on contemporary composers since Haydn's day. The
quartets written for Frederick William of Prussia are
an early instance, and Bernhard Romberg's fine playing (he wrote six concertos of his own) must have influenced Beethoven's cello writing, although Romberg
failed to appreciate Beethoven's music. Italian cello
technique lagged behind that of France, whose outstanding virtuoso, Servais, died in 1866 leaving cello
compositions with technical demands comparable to
those of Paganini. The underhand grasp of the bow
took longest to die in Italy but, in spite of this, an
Italian, Alfredo Piatti, became one of the most influen-
tial cello virtuosi of the nineteenth century. Pau Casals
has been responsible during the twentieth century for a
new appreciation of the cello's beauty as a solo instrument; and his revival of some older works, in particular
the six unaccompanied suites of Bach, has been accom-

panied by a renewal of interest in the instrument on the part of contemporary composers. Bloch, Delius, Elgar, Hindemith, Jacob, Khatchaturian, Milhaud and Walton have added to the repertoire for solo cello with orchestra: a similar increase in the sonata repertoire has been noted elsewhere. In concert hall, recital room, and chamber music the cellist today has a varied repertoire on which to draw, and a public which accepts and appreciates the instrument's solo qualities.

V. THE DOUBLE BASS

The lowest member of the violin family is the one with the least distinct ancestry and structural evolution. This is mainly because, although the upper members of the violin family were superior in tone to the viols, the double bass viol or violone was superior both in clarity of tone and in manageability to the clumsy gross-quint-bass, double bass of the violin family. Bach and his contemporaries preferred the violone, and the present double bass is the result of something of a compromise between the two. The violone is shown with high shoulders like the violin family in pictures as early as the seventeenth century; during the eighteenth century double basses were generally unfretted and varied in number of strings from four to six, their shape also varying from viol to violin, but the viol bow and method of bowing were invariably used. Tuning varied from fifths (derived from the violin family) to fourths and thirds (from the viols). A three-string bass, tuned in fourths or (more rarely) fifths was predominant during the early nineteenth century, but the practice of adding a fourth low string became gradually accepted as the demand for lower notes increased. In spite of Elgar's liking for the lowest sounds of the orchestra, England was apparently slow in taking to the four-string bass. A footnote to Alwyn's translation (1905) of Abele's book on the violin remarks 'This of course refers to the four-stringed double bass used in Germany, and not to the English three-stringed instrument'. The four-string bass is a less powerful instrument, but improved wood-wind and brass basses compensated for this. Occasionally today a fifth string is added at the bottom of the register to allow doubling of the complete cello range. This is not, however, a regular practice; it presents difficulties of construction if tuned a fourth lower than the bottom string, and difficulties of fingering if any other interval is used. The cog-wheel system has simplified the tuning of this unwieldy instrument, and a bow and bow technique similar to those of the cello were introduced by the double bass virtuoso Bottesini (1821-89), who gained astounding effects from his small, three-stringed Testore bass, of the type called a *basso da camera*, and composed fantasies and duets for his instrument.

The importance of the double bass to the string ensemble can easily be underestimated; one only needs to hear a string orchestra without basses to appreciate the extra resonance given to the tone by the 16 foot register. Composers were quick to realize this, and Bach and Handel gained variety by resting the basses or occasionally separating their line from that of the cellos. With the Mannheim symphonists the double basses mainly doubled bass lines, simplifying the difficult parts by playing one note in two or four. This simplification was probably used in Bach and Handel's orchestra as well: the standard of playing cannot have been very high during the early eighteenth century as only people who could cope with no other instrument were expected to play the bass at all. Quantz recommended frets on the double bass: to the objection that they interfered with the fingering of semitones he replied that there was little difference down there anyway!

During the lifetime of Haydn and Mozart a small version of the violin family's double bass, tuned in fourths, began to appear, and this more manageable instrument must have led to an improvement in orchestral bass technique. The great Dragonetti also led a fashion for solo double bass playing, and the early nineteenth century was probably the brightest period in the instrument's history, giving rise to double bass concertos by Haydn (now lost) and Dittersdorf (two, and one with viola).

The technical advances were soon reflected in orchestral writing. Beethoven's symphonies require an unprecedented technique and variety of expression from the basses, often quite independently of the cellos. Simplification by selecting notes from difficult passages is clearly not expected, because the basses are no longer invariably doubled even for difficult passage work, as we see in the Sixth and Ninth Symphonies. It would be difficult to remember any passage from a Mozart or Haydn symphony where the addition of basses to the cello line gives a special timbre, but several such passages leap to mind from Beethoven's symphonies; the fugato in the finale of number Five, the storm music from number Six, and the *quasi recitativo* from

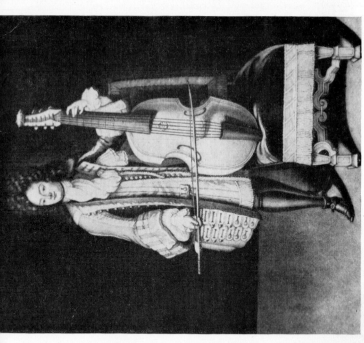

4. ST. CECILIA AND THE ANGEL

Carlo Saraceni 1585-1625

5. JOHANN SCHENK, viola da gamba virtuoso

mezzotint by his brother, Peter Schenk, 1645-1715

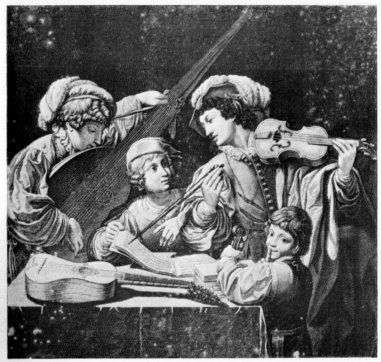

6. ENGRAVING BY PICART SHOWING AN ARCHLUTE OR CHITARRONE, GUITAR (on table) AND VIOLIN

From a painting by Domenico Zampieri (Domenichino)

Two ancestors of the modern double bass are shown on the previous page. The giant violin shape of the angel's instrument gave way to the more sloping shoulders of the viol; the sharp corners and overhanging back and belly are modified in various ways on modern instruments, the fingerboard has gradually lengthened, and the top of the back now slopes away towards the neck to increase the comfort and reach of the player. In Saraceni's picture the instrument already shows viol influence in its six strings, probably tuned like the viol; it is therefore not a true gross-quint-bass.

the finale of the Choral Symphony are some of the most obvious. Technical demands such as the passage work in the finale of the Fourth Symphony and the high leaps in the first movement exposition of the Choral must have necessitated a good deal of improvement on the part of Beethoven's contemporary bass players, and the triplets on double bass and double bassoon from *Fidelio* added a new colour to the orchestral palette.

The small bass used for solo work in this period was very gradually replaced by the more solid and powerful instrument we see in today's orchestra. Instead of the equal number of cellos and basses seen in most eighteenth-century orchestras, the bass section became smaller as it is today, and as weight and resonance was required by the nineteenth-century composers to balance the increasing use of brass instruments the larger bass was preferred to the more agile soloists' instrument. Technical developments in orchestral writing for the bass have thus been limited since Beethoven's time. The power and resonance of its pizzicato began to be exploited by Schubert, who used it in his Ninth Symphony for brief solo passages of imitation, and by Weber, who discovered the dramatic effect of pizzicato bass notes beneath a string tremolo. Rossini emphasizes the humorous aspect of the ungainly instrument in his youthful quartets, to be followed much later by Saint-Saëns' elephant. Mendelssohn set the seal on the fate of the third-rate performers with difficult passage-work like that in the *Hebrides* overture: divisi

E

basses were used effectively in the *William Tell* overture.

Berlioz recommends in his treatise that the basses
should always be doubled, but points out as an exception a passage in one of his cantatas, where double
basses, divided into four, play sustained pianissimo
chords to express 'lugubrious silence'. The variety of
tuning still prevalent is indicated in his suggestion that
some of the four-string basses should be tuned in fourths,
others in fifths and thirds, to give a greater variety of
open strings and harmonics.

Wagner, with his fondness for depth of tone, was
a champion of the four-string bass, and his use of it
was often particularly effective, one instance being the
persistent pianissimo unison with bass clarinet, horns
and trombones in Wotan's recitative from Act II of *Die
Walküre*. Tchaikovsky uses divisi basses with bassoons
for the opening of the Sixth Symphony, and Richard
Strauss gives the basses exciting, difficult parts to play.
One oboe solo from *Don Juan* has a background of
muted basses divided into four parts, with the third of
the chord omitted for clarity, and in *Also Sprach
Zarathustra* each of four desks plays a different part.
The sickening noise in Strauss's *Salome* while John the
Baptist's head is being cut off is made by the basses
bowing below the bridge. The composer's footnote to
the score points out that the sounds represent Salome's
maddened panting. Solo double bass passages are rare,
but they occur in Mahler's First, Fourth and Seventh
Symphonies, and in Elgar's Violin Concerto. A famous

solo for one desk of basses appears in Verdi's *Otello*; an ominous, heavy cantabile as Otello paces the bedroom.

The bass up to 1900 played a small part in chamber music, as its tone is too weighty to balance a small group; it appears in the larger ensembles, octet, septet, etc., Schubert's Trout Quintet and Dvořák's Sextet. George Onslow replaced the second cello of his four string quintets by a bass after hearing Dragonetti play, and modern composers such as Schoenberg and Stravinsky have made use in chamber music of the lighter effects given by a virtuoso technique.

Double bass parts today include passages which would have seemed very difficult even on the cello a hundred years ago. Debussy and, particularly, Ravel, made use of the bass's wide range of strong harmonics in their orchestral scores. Stravinsky's *Histoire du Soldat*, a chamber work with double bass, requires all kinds of technical feats with a particularly colourful use of harmonics; the symphonies of Sibelius and the double bass variation from Britten's *Young Person's Guide* show the potentialities of the orchestral group. Modern composers normally write for the four-string bass; it is a pity that the lower limit was not fixed earlier, for in passages such as the opening to Schubert's Unfinished Symphony the basses have to change from doubling at the octave to the unison, half-way through the phrase. It is unlikely that the five-string bass will be universally accepted, however, for the tradition of high technical standards on the four-string bass is flourishing everywhere. Fame such as that of Dragonetti, Bottesini, Lindley (who shared a desk in the orchestra with Dragonetti, it is said, for fifty-two years) Mori and Koussevitzky won on the small type of bass, is no longer customary, but the double bass has its outstanding players nationally if not internationally.

VI. CHAMBER MUSIC

Any composition with only one instrument to each part is, by present definition, chamber music. The string sonata with keyboard instrument has, however, sufficient interest to merit a chapter to itself; so we consider here ensembles of three or more instruments. Originally the description *musica da camera* indicated the place of performance rather than the number of players, but as *da camera* (for a room) became the accepted counterpart of *da chiesa* (for a church) the emphasis changed to the style of composition, secular or sacred. As these styles intermingled, orchestral works gradually ceased to be entitled chamber music, and small groups only have retained the title. True chamber music is a blending of equal voices to form an intimate, expressive whole; its performance is more suited to a room than to a concert hall, and even the pleasure of listening to it cannot rival that of playing it. Before the violins became popular, chamber music for viols was establishing this tradition of the 'music of friends'; particularly in England, where amateur string players would meet in groups to perform first the madrigals described as 'apt for voyces or viols', later, pieces specifically written for viol consort.

This early chamber music gave to each part an equal amount of interest and importance, a characteristic which was lost for a time as homophony (chordal writing) replaced polyphony (contrapuntal), to be gradually regained during the eighteenth century. The fantasias of Morley, Byrd and Gibbons are ideal for the amateur group of music makers; each part having melodic interest, but making limited technical demands on the performers. Ranging from two to six parts, they are usually made up of contrapuntal development of a single musical phrase, or several phrases, one being discarded as the next is taken up. Sometimes these phrases are contrasted and the work falls into sections like movements, as in Byrd's C minor Fantasia; Gibbons tended towards unity of his thematic material and thus approached the fugue. Other chamber music of the period, including *In Nomines* of church origin and dances which later formed the suite, makes enjoyable playing today, as long as the performers manage to imitate the smoothness, quietness, purity and ease of good viol tone.

England and France took the longest to accept the noisy violins into the intimate realm of chamber music : they appear to have crept in first by way of the secular dances. (The violin was for a long time considered more suited to the dancing-master and wedding-fiddler than the true music-maker.) Anthony Holborne's dances, published in 1599, are for 'viols, violins and other musical instruments', Dowland's *Lachrimae* (1604) also mentions violins. At the court of James I (1603-25) there were two violinists, Thomas Lupo and Davis Mell, and two composer-violists, Ferrabosco and Coperario (John Cooper, until a visit to Italy in the early years of the century caused him to change his name). Through them the Italian use of broken consorts—mixed viols and violins—was introduced into English chamber music. The Jacobean consort music in *Musica Britannica* (vol. 9) shows some idiomatic violin writing in the abstract chamber music, including leaping sequences of sevenths and ninths in Coperario's works, and Italian influence in the use of two violins with keyboard instrument and bass viol. William Lawes (1602-45) wrote for violins with theorbos, viols and harps or organ, but his music was for an ambitious court rather than for quiet music-making at home. John Jenkins (1592-1678) was, in later life, another English composer who really accepted the violin into chamber music; besides works for violins with other instruments, he composed trio fantasias for two violins and bass viol which are valuable as music in their own right and as clear precursors of Purcell's and Handel's compositions in this style.

In Italy, the violin became a chamber music instrument earlier than elsewhere. The practice of performing vocal music on instruments was followed by experiments with purely instrumental compositions, G. Gabrieli writing dramatic music for contrasted instrumental groups (following the tradition of antiphonal choral writing) while Salomone Rossi (1587-1628) and Biagio Marini (c. 1597-1665), a famous violinist, composed string chamber music. Rossi is associated with the emergence of the trio sonata, which soon became the most popular form of Italian chamber music, and

Marini popularized this form on his travels in Germany. Usually for four instruments—two violins, with a keyboard instrument and cello—the trio sonata was so named because only three parts were written down. The violin parts were written in full, but the cello (or bass viol) and keyboard shared a single line, with figures above or below the notes to indicate the harmonies to be filled in by the right hand of the keyboard player. This line was called the basso continuo, figured bass or thorough-bass, and a variety of instruments might be called upon to perform it: organ, harpsichord, harp, lute, bass viol, violone, cello, bassoon, and even, on occasions, viola. The title 'trio sonata' was justified only while the single-line continuo instrument doubled the keyboard bass throughout; soon four parts became audible as the cello broke away to make imitative entries in a higher register, and Telemann was quite accurate in calling some of his trio-sonata-type compositions 'quartets'.

Legrenzi (1626-90), and Corelli (1653-1713) in Italy, firmly established the trio sonata form in the church style (*sonata da chiesa*) and chamber style (*sonata da camera*). The former had abstract titles for its movements, (allegro, adagio) and was generally in three-part counterpoint, whereas the chamber sonata was the fore-runner of the suite in that its movements were dances and treated more homophonically. They are undoubtedly instrumental music, with no trace of vocal idiom; interesting to play today in spite of the limited range of the early violin. Different countries

absorbed the form and gave it a new aspect before
it died out; the trio sonatas of Purcell, for instance,
although composed in direct imitation of the Italian
style, have an unmistakable individuality. The Germans
tended to substitute the darker tone of the viola da
gamba for the second violin, but Bach left one sonata
for two violins and bass, three for violin, flute and
gamba, and the central section of the *Musical Offering*
which is a complete trio sonata for flute, violin and
bass. Handel's trio sonatas for various instruments are
pleasant to play: they show how by that time the
church and chamber styles had become mixed both in
the titles of movements and their degree of polyphony.

At this stage came a decided change in the style of
chamber music. It seems now entirely natural to speak
of the trio sonatas of composers up to the time of Bach
and Handel, and the string quartets of composers since
Haydn and Mozart. Yet Haydn wrote his first symphony
before Handel died; there is no long period of time in
which this complete change of style could have gradually taken place. The differences between the old and
the new style are considerable: two like instruments
and bass with a keyboard instrument to fill in the harmonies are replaced by four stringed instruments of
similar tone, providing complete harmonies without
support. The contrapuntal treatment of the two upper
parts, with continual crossing of parts and imitation,
gives way to homophonic writing with, at first, one
main melodic line in the first violin part; the three
movements become four, and the first movement

gains added length and importance by its treatment of two main themes in contrasted keys (sonata form) instead of a single subject.

Actually, several of these changes were being led up to by the composers of 1700-1750, but the emergence of the string quartet remains one of the most striking developments in musical history. The greatest change was the discarding of the continuo part, which took place first of all in chamber music, later in orchestral music and lastly in opera. The main factor contributing to its disappearance was the popularity, from about 1725, of a single melodic line with accompaniment, instead of the dignified contrapuntal complexity of the Baroque era. The employment of the first violin for the main melodic line left two stringed instruments to fill in the harmony, and the gap between them was more naturally filled by another member of the same family than by a keyboard instrument. The viola had already been used to supply the tenor contrapuntal voice in Baroque works; the *concertino* of Geminiani's concerti grossi, for instance, and even in some contrapuntal chamber works of A. Scarlatti and Allegri. Not until about 1745, however, did the complete string quartet emerge, to gain in importance until it held the supreme position in chamber music that it holds today.

The popularity of the divertimento, serenade and cassation (music for outdoor performance) during the eighteenth century must also have led to the decline in importance of the non-portable continuo instrument,

and to the inclusion of the minuet as a fourth movement. (Most serenades had several movements, generally with two minuets.) Matthias Monn first introduced the minuet into a symphony; Joseph Starzer
(1726-87) used only one minuet in his divertimenti for
strings without continuo.

The string orchestra and concertino group of Bach
and Handel's day seem to lead more directly to the
string quartet than any chamber ensemble of the time.
It is quite clear that the quartet did not originate from
the trio sonata with a viola replacing the keyboard
continuo. With the new chamber style came some
attributes of the Mannheim school of orchestral writing
and performing; contrasted moods within a movement
and carefully marked dynamics.

All these new characteristics are apparent in the
very first set of quartets by Haydn. The twelve quartets
of opus 1 and 2 are really divertimenti, with two
minuets each, and even additional horn parts to opus
1 no. 5. They were written for the four string players
at Count Fürnberg's residence, where Haydn was em-
ployed, and although he was at first thinking in terms
of a small divertimento orchestra rather than a string
quartet (the double basses are sometimes missed, when
crossing lower parts cause an incorrect progression)
Haydn's imagination must have been caught by the
possibilities of the ensemble, and he went on to develop
it to the full in his seventy-six quartets. Even the earliest
quartets give a certain amount of interest to the lower
parts, differing in this respect from the trio sonata and

the contemporary symphony. The frequent doubling of two parts in octaves was a divertimento feature appearing in the early quartets, an occasional slip such as a pause on a bare 4th indicates that Haydn may be relying on a continuo. The lower parts never become mere accompaniments except in a few slow movements, and this is where Haydn's earliest quartets stand apart from anything which had gone before and assume the title of the first true string quartets. Sammartini and Tartini may have produced earlier works for four strings, but they lack the element of dialogue which is a basic ingredient of chamber music.

From opus 3 onwards the quartets of Haydn have four movements, and they show a steady expansion in length, content and instrumental treatment. Gradually the cello ceases to merely provide the bass line, and all three lower instruments take a turn in discussing the material. The quartets of opus 20 introduce the polyphonic element, and the four instruments necessarily gain an equal status in the fugal finales. A ten-year gap in his quartet composing prefaced Haydn's next set—the 'Russian' quartets (dedicated to the Grand Duke Paul of Russia), opus 33. He described them as being written 'in an entirely new and special manner', and they show a new ease in the development of melodic fragments of the subject matter. The minuets are labelled *scherzo* for the first time; the instruments are almost equal participants in all discussion, although, with Haydn, the first violin always retains a certain superiority of position. The opus 50 quartets give a new precedence to the cello because they are dedicated to King Frederick William II, a cellist, and opus 50 and opus 64 show an increased use of the chromatic line, evidence of Mozart's influence at that time. The peak of Haydn's achievement in this field was reached with his opus 76 and opus 77, including the famous 'Emperor', 'Quinten' and 'Sunrise' quartets, but any one of them, from opus 1 no. 1 to opus 77, no. 2, can give both performer and listener the conviction that a string quartet is chamber music's most natural medium.

Few instrumental composers since Haydn and Mozart have failed to add to the string quartet repertoire, which includes a comparatively large number of really great works; Beethoven's later quartets, Schubert's 'Death and the Maiden', the three of Brahms, to name a few. The great nineteenth-century quartets use mainly a single line technique from all four players, expecting an equal ability to cope with high positions (although the first violin, naturally, is apt to rise the highest) and passage-work, but rarely applying virtuoso techniques, multiple stops, fancy bowings and harmonics. These would have seemed out of character in what has always been considered one of the most serious and intimate musical forms: not until Debussy were the expressive qualities of some virtuoso string effects recognized and used in serious quartet writing.

Since the Müller Brothers' String Quartet left the service of the Duke of Brunswick in 1831 and toured Europe, a fine tradition of professional quartet-playing has flourished in Europe and America. When one considers that the four players must match in technique, temperament, instrument, interpretation, and every other way except in appearance, it seems remarkable that so many fine quartets—the Amadeus, Busch, Griller, Hollywood, Italian, Joachim, for instance— spring to mind.

Other ensembles first used in the eighteenth century matured less rapidly and have received less attention since, as each of them produces greater problems of balance than the string quartet. The string trio was given some similar qualities to Haydn's quartets in Boccherini's early works: trio playing requires greater virtuosity from all the performers than quartet playing, double stops are frequent and bad intonation painfully apparent, but a fine performance of Mozart's Divertimento, a trio by Beethoven or a more modern work such as the Serenade of Dohnányi will reveal that the group has great possibilities. Duets, whatever the instruments concerned, normally give more pleasure to the performer than the listener: perhaps those of Mozart for violin and viola are an exception, but although Beethoven wrote for viola and cello, these works stand almost alone as valuable representatives of a form of composition, in the same way as Dvořák's Terzetto for two violins and viola.

The string quintet has received more attention. Locatelli discovered the richness of sound given by a concertino of two violins, two violas and cello in his concerti grossi, and Mozart, Beethoven and Brahms used the same group in chamber music. Boccherini, a cellist, added an extra cello to the string quartet so that the first cello could soar to virtuoso heights without having to worry about providing a bass line : Schubert used the same group to gain magnificent colours in his C major Quintet. Larger groups of strings alone are used for certain isolated masterpieces such as the two Brahms Sextets and the Mendelssohn Octet.

An early intruder into the realm of string chamber music was the harpsichord, followed by the pianoforte. Banished from its former supporting position, it returned with a firm conviction of its right to monopolize the interest, as we see in Haydn's trios. The balance of the eighteenth-century trios is lost today owing to the resonance of the modern, felt-hammered, iron-framed pianoforte, which drowns the string tone in comparison with the plucked harpsichord or the leather-hammered fortepiano of Haydn and Mozart. Even under the right conditions, however, only one or two piano trios before Beethoven are chamber music in that the material is shared fairly with the stringed instruments. Beethoven, Mendelssohn, Schumann and Brahms showed that a balance is possible between violin, cello and piano, and many composers have added to the repertoire : Schubert's B flat Trio is one of his greatest works.

The three strings of the piano quartet provide a complete group suitable for antiphonal writing, and would seem to present fewer problems of balance than the piano trio. After the fine first two works by Mozart, the group was not very frequently written for; Brahms and Schumann wrote piano quartets but Fauré was perhaps the most at home in the medium among the nineteenth-century composers. Romantic composers preferred to add another violin: Brahms, Franck, Elgar and Schumann wrote for the piano quintet thus formed, and used previously by Boccherini, but Schubert preferred to add a double bass in his 'Trout' Quintet.

In performing works for piano and strings, balance has to be carefully considered in order to preserve the chamber style of intimacy and equality; it is all too easy to give the impression of an accompanied piano piece. Chamber music with wind instruments presents further problems for the string player, who must strive to match the incisiveness of an oboist's attack, the round fulness of horn tone or the quietness and agility of a flute; the clarinet seems the easiest instrument to come to terms with.

The technique required of string players for most nineteenth-century chamber music underwent little change apart from an upward extension of the range of the lower instruments. Styles of writing varied greatly, but the actual sounds required were fairly constant until Debussy's Quartet appeared in 1893. The effects required in this work were entirely different from any previous chamber music: it is exciting to play and listen to today, and it baffled his contemporaries for a time. The equality of parts is apparent in a new way; each instrument in turn has a chance to bring out the melody, often with effective doublings such as viola with second violin on the G string, but it must learn to discard its individuality in creating an atmosphere in the accompaniment passages: the murmuring scales near the beginning are an instance of where the notes and the instruments playing them are of less importance than the effect of a misty background to the melody. This does not mean that any less accuracy is required from the players, (the slightest failure in ensemble or intonation will make those semiquavers resemble smog rather than mist), but the bow stroke used must vary from the lightest flautando to the greatest intensity, and the vibrato from none at all (rare in chamber music playing) to a passionate warmth. Chords with double and triple stops in all parts provide striking contrasts, and in this and Ravel's Quartet the new colours require new and more advanced technique: octaves, harmonics, trills and tremolos, very high positions. The second violinist can no longer sit back and relax because he is not leading; he certainly has the most difficult part in the first movement of Debussy's Quartet!

Modern chamber music has tended to become technically so difficult that it is far beyond the reach of amateurs; thus it loses one of its most important characteristics, enjoyment through performance. The quartets of Berg and Schoenberg present major technical problems even to professional groups; as early as 1899, in his string sextet *Verklärte Nacht* Schoenberg had revealed the wide variety of textures obtainable through combinations of muted, unmuted, pizzicato, tremolo

F

and double-stopped strings, and with ethereal echo effects in false and natural harmonics; his later works are more difficult in that they are further from the nineteenth-century traditions of string technique. Bartók's six quartets seem between them to contain every possible sound effect, often to increase rhythmic or harmonic percussiveness; each appears to be more difficult than its predecessor. Glissandi from one note to another, with or without vibrato on the way, are later required from one three note chord (pizzicato) to another, and from all four instruments at once. Guitar-like and 'snap' pizzicato, quarter tones, col legno, and extremely difficult triple and quadruple stops are used frequently and effectively. Britten's Second Quartet shows the intrusion of virtuoso writing into chamber music in its cadenza for the first violin (although one must not forget a much earlier instance in the Beethoven Septet).

As the article on chamber music in Grove points out, 'Chamber music combinations, and particularly the string quartet, have been found to be a peculiarly convenient medium for all those experiments with atonality, polytonality, quarter-tones and other divisions of the scale which are characteristic of the restless technical enterprise of today.' Performers of some of the least orthodox modern string works are apt to get the impression that the individuality of their instruments and the quality of the ensemble has ceased to count: that an electronic reproduction of the notes might more nearly approach the composer's requirements. Perhaps the time will come when a string quartet will gain as much pleasure from performing one of Webern's quartets as one of Mozart's, but at present the extreme difficulty and elusiveness of effect of this type of composition must exclude all but the most expert.

Counterbalancing this growth of technical complexity, however, we find certain twentieth-century composers writing chamber music which asks to be played, and which frequently extends the repertoire of rather neglected ensembles. The night that the violin and viola are left on their own, for instance, need no longer be spent solely on the two duos of Mozart and odd trifles of his lesser contemporaries: Halvorsen, Gordon Jacob and Martinů have given them interesting works to explore. Another violin or a cello will make possible the trio of Kodály or Dohnányi, a flute may be added for Reger's trio for violin, flute and viola. The non-professional string quartet seeking to play some modern music may well enjoy some of the works of Milhaud and Rubbra, while the addition of wind opens the way for Gordon Jacob's Oboe Quartet, Sir Arthur Bliss's Quintet for clarinet and strings, and Lennox Berkeley's Horn Trio. The day that eight players are gathered beneath one roof for a Beethoven Septet-Schubert Octet evening should be regarded as an opportunity for sampling Howard Ferguson's Octet: by seeking out and enjoying those works which are practicable for non-professional musicians, the amateur can extend his understanding and appreciation of the modern chamber music which is technically beyond his grasp.

VII. THE STRING SONATA

The sonata of today for stringed instrument and pianoforte is a piece of chamber music, and the two participants must approach it on equal terms. Although this has not always been the case, a certain individuality and independence of the parts, even when the interest was very unevenly divided, has been one of the distinguishing characteristics of the string sonata since its emergence in the second decade of the seventeenth century. In the earliest solo sonatas, the violin certainly predominated, but the continuo part was given contrapuntal interest so that the work did not become a solo with accompaniment. Occasional works entitled *sonata* which have no interest in the bass are really solos in the monodic vocal style.

Various sources have been suggested for the duet sonata. Diego Ortiz (in his treatise on ornamentation, 1553) gives instructions for performance of a madrigal or motet on the harpsichord with one of the parts (omitted by the harpsichord) played, with ornamentation, on a viol. This would give duet sonata instrumentation, as would Christopher Simpson's instructions for playing divisions on a ground, when a treble instrument devised counterpoint over a bass while the gamba was free to add interest to the bass line itself.

The popularity during the late sixteenth and early seventeenth centuries of vocal duets or *bicinia* may also have led towards the duet sonata, as the second part was frequently performed on an instrument. A clearer derivation is from the trio sonata: it is often easy to see how the two violin parts have been condensed into one, in Corelli's solo sonatas, for instance. Imitative entries are contrived by double stops and by contrasts of register, passages in thirds and sixths by breaking the chords into shorter time values. Apart from this conscious contraction, by the composer, of two parts into one, the violin began to dominate in the trio sonata when a lower instrument replaced the second violin, assuming a part like that of the continuo because of its inability to rival the violin's brilliant tone. A further connection between trio sonata and duet sonata was seen when the second treble-instrument part was transferred to the right hand of the keyboard, as in Biagio Marini's opus 8 (1626), a violin sonata with the organ part written out.

Just as the trio sonata normally involved four players, so the early solo sonata was played by three, a keyboard instrument and cello, lute or bass viol sharing the figured bass. The title *da chiesa* was rarely used with a solo sonata, although it is easy to distinguish the church style in, for instance, the first six of Corelli's opus 5; he uses double stops to give the contrapuntal voice effect. Marini and Fontana were pioneers of the violin sonata: with Corelli it gained a dignity and consistency which has made some of his works in the form retain popularity until today. The German composers, Biber and Walther, made great technical strides in their violin sonatas, particularly in the direction of high positions and double stops. They frequently varied the tuning of the strings to facilitate stops (scordatura); this tendency was of course leading away from the equality of parts which is characteristic of the later sonata.

The Italian virtuosi, led in this field by Tartini, also tended to develop the violin part with little regard to the continuo, and performers were free to embellish the parts as they went along. Modern performances of the bare notes, as written, would probably sound most unnatural to the composers of the seventeenth and early eighteenth centuries; many of the slow movements of Corelli, Vivaldi and Handel are merely sketches to be ornamented *ad libitum*. C. P. E. Bach, Quantz, and Geminiani have left detailed descriptions of how this was done, and some modern editors have written out probable decorations, but it seems a pity that the art of free embellishment, like that of improvising a cadenza, should have died.

For a time the sonata was almost monopolized by violinist-composers, some of them pupils of Corelli, who expanded and varied his form. Geminiani, Locatelli and Tartini gave their first movements greater length and dignity (Tartini's 'Devil's Trill' sonata is a good example), while their final movements began to show key contrasts leading to sonata form. The second movement retained its moderately quick fugal pattern, the third was slow and expressive. The *sonata da camera* was no longer apparent, as the use of dances had passed mainly to the suite and partita, but the last movements were occasionally in dance forms. The four-movement form was not used exclusively; Locatelli frequently omitted the slow opening movement and ended with an aria and variations on a ground bass; Tartini sometimes used a three movement form, and Nardini wrote six sonatas in three movements each beginning with a slow movement.

This early type of solo sonata reached its highest musical value with Bach and Handel; the latter following Corelli's pattern in his six violin sonatas, all of which are effectively written for the violin and contain some interest in the continuo part. Bach, like Marini, wrote out the right hand of the keyboard part of his six sonatas. (William Lawes had also written out full continuo parts for his chamber works in the previous century.) His main texture is polyphonic, like the trio-sonata with the upper two parts crossing. Occasionally the keyboard has chords, or the violin double stops, and the slow movements of the E major sonata are exceptional; the violin having free arabesques over a fuller chordal figuration in the accompaniment of the adagio. The word *accompagnando* (appearing, for instance, in the fifth sonata) indicates that Bach required some additional improvisation in the keyboard part, and although the three parts appear to be balanced without support, allowance was made in the title of an autograph manuscript for *an Optional Accompanying Bass Viola da Gamba*. Other works for violin and keyboard, rarely performed, include a Suite and a Fugue in G minor; three sonatas for gamba are played today on the viola or cello.

Original sonatas for viola and continuo were not written up to this time owing to the lack of interest in, and performers on, the instrument. The cello fared better, although the sonatas of D. Gabrieli, Attilio Ariosti, Bononcini and Batistini Stuck have not remained in the repertoire like the contemporary violin sonatas. The opinion of Quantz was that 'Solo-playing on this instrument is not an easy matter', and little of musical value was written for cello and keyboard before 1750, although some viol sonatas sound effective on the cello.

The Baroque solo sonata did not lead directly to the classical duet sonata by a gradual expansion of the keyboard part, as one might expect. While Tartini was carrying on the tradition of a dominating, technically brilliant violin part in his sonatas, C. P. E. Bach was developing the sonata for solo keyboard instrument, and Mozart's earliest duet sonatas were written in C. P. E. Bach's form and entitled *Clavierduetti with Violin*, or *for Harpsichord or Pianoforte with Violin accompaniment*. Often the violin part could be omitted without much loss, but in Mozart's later sonatas the two instruments begin to share the material in the true chamber music style which has been a characteristic of the duet sonata ever since. The little E minor sonata (K.304), the B flat (K.454) and the A major (K.526) are among the most frequently heard and the most satisfying to play from the violinist's point of view; but any of the later sonatas will repay a careful study of balance and phrasing as the melodic material is passed from one instrument to the other. Both violin and piano have increased in power since these sonatas were written; the pianist has also to remember that a modern piano lacks the clarity of Mozart's fortepiano with leather-covered hammers.

Beethoven and his successors wrote for instruments similar to those in use today, but in duet sonatas the pianist has to keep in mind the size and power of an iron-framed piano compared with a violin, viola or cello. The violin presents the least problem owing to its high pitch and sustaining power, but the violinist has more difficulty in blending an accompanying passage with the piano than the two lower instruments. Various methods have been used to give a balanced effect in the string sonata, apart from Mozart's alternation of melody and accompaniment in each part: Beethoven twice (in the Cello Sonata opus 69 and the Kreutzer Violin Sonata) opens the work with an unaccompanied string statement, echoed by the piano, thus asserting their equality from the outset. In the Kreutzer Sonata the two instruments gain equality through virtuosity: the last violin sonata (no. 10: opus 96) and the late cello sonatas (opus 102, nos. 1 and 2) obtain a closer relationship with less display. The music seems no longer to be shared out between the two instruments, but to have grown up inevitably for the medium; and the contrapuntal aspect is strongly emphasized— the last movement of opus 102, no. 2 being a three-part fugue. The cello is used effectively in both its low and its high register, but any of these sonatas can be ruined by a lack of discretion on the part of the pianist.

A new way of preserving the equality of status of two contrasted instruments appeared in the first movement of César Franck's Violin Sonata, which gives the piano entirely different material from the violin. This effective sonata balances two movements in which the piano is slightly more prominent by a *Recitativo-Fantasia* for the violin, and concludes with the two instruments on terms of complete equality in a canonic finale. Economy of notes in the piano part makes some works (the violin sonatas of Debussy, Ravel and some modern composers such as Aaron Copland, for instance) easier to perform from the point of view of balance; Ravel's and Kodály's sonatas for violin and cello are interesting works which overcome even greater problems of medium. The outstanding contributor to string sonata literature after Beethoven was Brahms, who wrote three violin and two cello sonatas, all of which are frequently heard. Their technical demands on the stringed instruments are not as great as the sonatas of Fauré or Franck, but they require considerable sonority of tone to match the rich piano writing—Pizzetti and Elgar demand a similar fulness of tone in their violin sonatas.

The cello sonata repertoire was increased during the nineteenth century by several enjoyable if not great works; Mendelssohn, Schumann, Chopin, Rubinstein, Grieg, Saint-Saëns and Strauss all wrote for cello with piano, sometimes in shorter forms than the sonata. In the twentieth century, two late cello sonatas of Fauré, and one by Debussy gave a lead followed by Shostakovich, Kodály, Hindemith, Britten and many others; there is no longer an excuse for including one of the four most popular sonatas of Beethoven and Brahms as the sole sonata item of every cello recital.

Brahms arranged his two clarinet sonatas (opus 120) for violin and piano, but they are more often heard as viola sonatas, as the violist has a poor selection of nineteenth-century works. Schubert's sonata for arpeggione (an obsolete instrument, a cross between cello and guitar) sounds well on the viola : some earlier works by Flackton are valuable for their antiquity; the remainder of the viola sonata repertoire belongs mainly to the twentieth century. Reger and Hindemith have each provided several works; Milhaud, Bax, Arthur Benjamin, Bliss and others have proved the viola as suitable for the duet sonata as the violin and cello. Hindemith and Sprongl are almost alone in attempting a balance between double bass and piano, but it seems no less worthy of consideration than a concerto for tuba or harmonica would have seemed, earlier this century.

Each member of the violin family has been occasionally considered capable of unaccompanied performance, although they are naturally single-line instruments. Pisendel, Matteis and Geminiani followed Farina, Marini and Biber in writing for violin alone, but only Bach's compositions for solo violin and solo cello have remained in the repertoire. Among more recent unaccompanied compositions are those of Kreisler, Ysaÿe, Bartók, Prokofiev, Honegger, and Nielsen for the violin; Reger and Hindemith for the viola, and Reger and Kodály for cello. Unaccompanied strings in pairs or groups of the same member of the family have occasionally provided an interesting experimental medium; Villa-Lobos has used a group of cellos, Dubensky a group of basses, but the difficulty of finding the requisite number of performers at one time makes this type of ensemble a rarity.

The string sonata has, like the quartet, tended to require a technique beyond the reach of amateur performers in the twentieth century, which is a loss both to the amateur performer and to the composer, whose appreciative public is reduced by a small but important section. An amateur violinist enjoys most a fine performance of a work he has played; any good work is appreciated more when it is thoroughly familiar than at a first hearing. Perhaps the most playable of recent sonatas have the best chance of survival—Tchaikovsky's Violin Concerto is still very much alive although it was considered impossible at the time it was written, but concertos are for virtuosi, whereas sonatas like all other chamber music, belong as much to the amateur as to the professional.

VIII. THE STRUCTURE OF THE VIOLIN

The violin seems to have combined the best points of several earlier families of stringed instruments, but to have derived directly from none of them. It has an oval sound-chest, with a vaulted belly and back which slightly overhang the narrow ribs. The arched back and belly (obtained by carving them from a thick board with gouges and small curved planes) appear to have been derived from the lyra da braccio, an instrument popular in the late fifteenth century. The tone of a violin is considerably affected by the curve of its back and belly, a high arch giving a brighter, softer tone while a moderate arch gives more power. Usually both back and belly are made in two pieces of wood with a join down the centre: the belly from pine or fir wood of varying grain (but old Italian violins rarely have a very close grain), the back and ribs from maple. Occasionally poplar wood is used for the back of a cello or double bass.

A short distance from the edge of both back and belly is inserted the purfling, a narrow strip made of three slips of wood, two dyed black and the middle one white, glued together and inserted into a groove cut into the board. This is said to increase the elasticity of the board and to strengthen the overhanging edges. Whalebone purflings are sometimes used (Nicolas Lupot always used whalebone) and occasional decorative purflings are found on old violins, such as the 'Greffuhle' violin of Stradivari which has its edges inlaid with little diamond-shaped ivory plates. Maggini often used a double purfling.

Several precursors of the violin family have a sound-chest with ribs, and some which started life with a flat belly and strongly curved back, giving a half-pear shape, later adopted a flat back and front joined by ribs, like the present guitar. The vielle made this change *c.* 1300, probably for convenience, as it was played in violin position, unlike the pear-shaped rebec which was then rested on the knee. The viol family had very deep ribs which were not overhung by the back and belly, and like the violins, had supporting blocks of light willow or lime wood in the corners of the C-curves. These curves began to appear in the twelfth century, when the popularity of drone strings was waning and musicians began to play on one string alone. They gradually deepened to allow greater freedom of bowing, and even appeared unnecessarily on certain plucked instruments such as the guitar, which still retains an incurved waist. Because of this waist on the plucked instruments, it has been suggested that the shape derives from the lyre, but the fact remains that it is impossible to bow on a single string of an unwaisted, broad instrument.

The thin maple from which violin ribs are made is strengthened by linings glued inside, making a strong air-tight connection between back and belly. Besides the four corner-blocks, two more blocks give support; one at the top to support the neck, the other at the bottom to take the weight of tail-pin and saddle. The sound-post, (a cylindrical piece of hard maple about a quarter of an inch thick, connecting back and belly close to the E-string foot of the bridge) is there not for support, but to transmit vibrations to the back and keep them similar throughout the sound-chest. This is only necessary in bowed instruments, which sustain the tone; plucked instruments would be hindered by a sound-post—a fact made apparent from the weakness of violin pizzicato.

The bass bar, a piece of specially matured pine running inside the belly for about two-thirds of its length, parallel to the strings and beneath the left (G string) foot of the bridge, transmits the long vibrations of the lower notes. Fifteenth- and sixteenth-century instruments possessed both sound-post and bass-bar, (although the latter has become considerably longer), and the early recognition of the need for a sound-post in bowed instruments is shown in the crwth, which has one foot of the bridge passing through a hole in the belly to the back. Bass-bars deteriorate and need replacing approximately every twenty years, more frequently when metal strings are used.

The f-shaped sound holes of the violin family distinguish it from the viol family which have C-shaped ones; the shape is not accidental, but the result of the arch of the belly. Their function is to give elasticity to the soundboard, to enable it to vibrate freely so that its vibrations may be carried to the rest of the sound-chest. Without sound-holes, the belly could not support the 26lb. vertical tension of the strings on the bridge. The position of violin sound-holes allows the belly to vibrate at the moment a note is sounded, but eliminates after-vibrations: instruments which require prolonged vibration like the lute have a circular sound-hole known as a 'rose'. The ancient Egyptians used sound-holes on the back as well as the belly, and since their time innumerable shapes and sizes of sound-hole have been used, sometimes detracting from instead of adding to the tone of an instrument, as in the case of the rebec which received the rose suitable for plucked instruments. The violin f-hole has, however, been a characteristic feature since its first emergence.

The bridge is placed between the f-holes, at the highest point of the belly. Made of maple, its graceful shape is said to have been originated by Stradivari, and it can strongly influence the tone of the instrument. It is sufficiently arched to allow free bowing on each string, and is kept in position by the pressure of the strings. The two feet leave the central join of the belly free, and pass their vibrations to the sound-post and bass-bar. Several earlier instruments than the violins adopted an arched bridge to eliminate the drone of the other strings, rubebe and fiedel among them; in the violin family the height of the arch was increased when the bass-bar was lengthened, with the desire for greater volume *c*. 1800.

With a higher bridge naturally came an alteration in the angle of the fingerboard, so that at about this time most violins had their necks removed and replaced by longer ones, thrown back at an angle instead of continuing in the plane of the belly. The short fingerboard of Corelli's time only allowed the use of low positions, and as technique advanced the fingerboard gradually had to be lengthened; there has been no further change, however, since the early nineteenth century.

Violins imitated the rebec and differed from the viols in discarding the gut frets tied round the neck. The neck, peg-box and scroll are usually made of maple, the fingerboard of ebony, and the width of the neck is determined by the four strings: the early violins had an advantage in left hand agility over their thicker-necked rivals, the six-stringed instruments. In the earliest instruments (a fingerboard instrument is shown in an illustration dating from *c*. 2500 B.C. at Nippur, but harps were more common in ancient civilizations) the neck and body were often made in one piece; some, like the rebec, clung to this tradition and therefore fell out of use because of the awkwardness of their left hand technique.

Awkwardness in handling caused some forms of peg-box to be rejected; the slightly thrown back one of the violin was derived from the rebec, which probably copied it originally from the mandola. The first vielles had the pegs inserted into a board in the same plane as the fingerboard, but this vertical position was later changed to the more convenient one with the pegs inserted sideways into a peg-box and therefore lying parallel to the belly. Greater tension was obtained by

G

throwing the peg-box back at a slight angle in the mandola and at 90° in the lute, but the right-angle was found to be awkward for instruments resting on the shoulder when the rebec began to be played in this way, and the mandola peg-box was adopted by most bowed instruments. The scroll of the violin replaced the carved human or animal head of the rebec; viols used either scroll or head. Some are illustrated on p. 122.

The strings of the modern violin family are made from metal, gut, or gut wound with metal: they became a little longer and more taut when violins were altered to accommodate a general rise in pitch and volume towards the end of the eighteenth century. Metal strings with woven, flexible cores, and nylon strings are being experimented with. Possibly hemp was first used for musical instruments, although sheep gut was also common in Old Testament times. Fibre, silk and horse-hair have also been used, and wire since it was first made in fourteenth-century Nuremberg. Metal E strings, with an adjuster attached to the tail-piece to give greater accuracy in tuning, are a comparatively recent development, for early in the twentieth century the preparation and selection of gut E strings was considered a topic worthy of several pages of discussion in a German book on the violin. Italian gut E strings were acknowledged to be the finest, essentials of preparation being warmth of climate, and the use of entrails of young, thin animals.

The tuning of the violin family in fifths points to the rebec as an ancestor: some of the earliest violas had only three strings, tuned in fifths, but soon a fourth was normally added, so that the instrument was tuned as the viola today. The tenor (now extinct) and bass (cello) of the family were tuned each a fifth lower; some fifty years later the violin emerged tuned a fifth above the viola. Other off-shoots of the family, to be described later, adopted different tunings. The cello was generally called *violoncello* by 1700; about this time it began to be tuned a tone higher, at its present pitch, and the dimensions correspondingly decreased. The double bass violin or gross-quint-bass, as it was called, was most adversely affected by the tuning in fifths, as the stop was too large for the comfortable filling in of three notes between the open strings. This fact, combined with its great size and the coarseness of its strings led to a general preference for the violone.

The strings of the violin family are attached to a tail-piece of ebony or rose-wood, sometimes ornamented, which is held by a loop of thick gut round the tail-pin. On the violin, an adjuster is generally used for the fine tuning of the E string: if all the strings are metal, a special tail-piece has been designed with an adjuster for each string. A type of tail-piece appeared as early as the tenth century, on the small vielle: previous to this a string-holder attached to the table of the instrument was used, as in the guitar.

None of the component parts of the violin was without a predecessor, yet the instrument was so superior to its bowed contemporaries as to have survived alone to the present day: who originated the design, no one knows. Some claim that Gasparo Duiffoprugghar (or Duiffoprogar, or Dieffenbrucker, or Tieffenbrucker) made the first violins, but the first eminent violin maker was Gasparo Bertolotti da Salo (1540-1609) who taught Maggini. Their instruments are beautifully made but have small carrying power. The old violins which are so highly rated today were mainly made at Cremona by the school founded by Andrea Amati, and continued by his two sons Antonio and Girolamo, whose son Nicolò became the most eminent member of the family. Nicolò taught Antonio Stradivari (1645-1737) who made larger, flatter violins, more powerful than the Amatis but just as sweet in tone. The third great master of the Cremona school was Giuseppe Guarneri (1687-1742), whose genius was recognized by Paganini. Later famous Italian makers included the Testore family of Milan, the Guadagnini family of Piacenza and Turin, and the Gagliano family of Naples. Other countries produced their own famous makers, and their instruments have a characteristic tone which is generally easy to distinguish from Italian tone; Stainer of the Tyrol, the Klotz family of Mittenwald and Lupot of Paris made violins of wide repute.

In spite of the general acceptance of violin structure on the Italian pattern, attempts have been made to improve on it, and to enlarge the family. Although none of the new styles of instrument have won popular acceptance, they have proved that the traditional pattern is not the only one to give good results; tests carried out with performances on old Italian and new model violins, hidden from the audience, have even produced a majority in favour of the new shape. Chanot believed that the violin's corners were detrimental to the tone, and from 1817 he built instruments in the approximate shape of the guitar, but although their tone was good they never became popular. Savart of Paris produced a trapezoid box-fiddle which gave good tone (1819), and Stelzner of Dresden (*c.* 1890) made several successful instruments with all curves part of the parabola or the ellipse, including the violotta, a large, deep viola which was too uncomfortable to play. His cellona, tuned a fourth lower than the cello and intended for chamber music, met with as little success as Vuillaume's octobass (1849), a three-stringed bass of such mammoth proportions that the strings had to be stopped by levers worked by pedals, designed to give thirty-two foot tone to the orchestra.

Various attempts were made to fill the gap between viola and cello by an instrument held under the chin or between the legs—such as Ritter's five-stringed viola alta, used by Wagner at Bayreuth, and Parramon's violeténor, held between the knees, and praised by Casals and Ravel—but although they attracted the attention of a few composers, none have persisted. A slightly larger violin for playing second violin parts called a contra-violin was introduced by Newbould, 1917; this too has died. Some of the supposedly obsolete members of the violin family can still be heard today, however; the tiny kit or dancing master's violin, tuned an octave above the violin, has not been revived, but the violino piccolo may be heard, tuned a third above the violin, in some modern performances of Bach's first Brandenburg Concerto.

The viola d'amore, a viol-like instrument played like the violin, without frets, but with a set of sympathetic metal strings close to the belly which gave a soft, affecting tone, was very popular in the eighteenth century, and has never truly died out. Works for it have been written by Vivaldi, Ariosti, Bach, Handel, Berlioz, Meyerbeer, Loeffler, and Richard Strauss, while proof of its survival into the present century lies in the sonata and concerto by Hindemith. In England the viola d'amore was sometimes called a violet. Another many-stringed instrument which has died is the viola di bordone, or baryton, for which Haydn composed one hundred and seventy sonatas because it was the favourite instrument of his patron, Prince Esterházy. The extreme concentration necessary to bow and finger a melody while plucking the accompaniment with the thumb of the left hand on a set of strings behind the neck of the instrument contributed to its rapid downfall.

Present experiments tend towards the analysis of the construction of fine old instruments, so as to reproduce them as accurately as possible, rather than attempt at a radical change of shape. It seems unlikely that after four centuries of ever-increasing popularity the present pattern of the violin family will be ousted by a newcomer.

IX. THE BOW AND BOWING

The modern bow of the violin family is designed to give the performer the maximum control over the vibration of the strings and therefore the greatest variety in tonal effect. Position, pressure and pace (the invaluable 'three p's' for teaching purposes) of the bow; its rugosity, and the thickness of string in relation to the bow, all affect the tonal quality: the expert violinist is capable of producing an infinite variety of tonal colours by varying the proportion of these sound-producing factors. Greater pressure with less speed of bow travel, for instance, will give more intensity to the sound. The bow pressure is a result of the simple lever produced by the downward pressure of the performer's index finger on the bow, the thumb acting as fulcrum and the pressure on the string the work done.

This is an over-simplified picture, as it does not take into account the natural 'give' of a ribbon of horse-hairs suspended between two terminals of a tapering stick, which has a negative (towards the hair) curve, lessened but far from eliminated when the hairs are under tension. Practically, however, it provides the basis for the string player's regulation of pressure, and he adjusts his first finger pressure sufficiently to gain an even tone over the whole length of the bow when pace and position remain constant.

The flat hair is not invariably used, the bow being tilted slightly away from the bridge for some types of playing. This angle of attack is particularly important in producing varying degrees of staccato bowing, as the sideways pressure causes the bow to 'whip', a factor utilized by the skilful player.

The earliest bows clearly depicted (in Serrano Fatigati's tenth-century *Miniaturas de códices españoles*) resemble more closely the bow-and-arrow type of bow than our modern stick. Primitive types of instrument still used today in various parts of the world retain these characteristics of the earliest bows; a semicircular type held at the middle, and a demi-semicircular type held at one end. Until the fourteenth century the only change appeared to be an extension of one end of the second type to form a handle. The cheerful musicians and musical angels in fourteenth and fifteenth-century paintings have ceased to use the semicircular bow, but their bow grip shows infinite variety: some clutch the handle firmly, like a tennis racquet, others use two fingers above and two below the stick; occasionally, the grip bears some resemblance to the modern practice. During the sixteenth century, the nut appeared; this controlled the hair tension and provided a grip. Sixteenth-century pictures show that the viol bowing method, with the thumb above the stick, was becoming the general rule for instruments held downwards.

Later in the century, the ferrule began to appear in paintings, and the bow became less convex, especially that of the violin; the viol bow was more curved for chordal playing. By the mid-seventeenth century the stick for both families was almost straight, and instead of tapering to a point it began gradually to develop a 'nose', an important feature of the modern bow. Early in the eighteenth century the bow was given a wider space between the hair and the wood, the two being almost parallel as the nut and the nose are of equal depth. Before the screw became the accepted method of adjusting string tension, a toothed piece of metal was sometimes placed above the heel to which the nut could be attached with a loop of wire, thus varying the hair tension according to the tooth used. As the bow was held some distance from the nut (bow wrappings and engravings indicate that this was the custom until *c.* 1800), this would cause no discomfort to the performer. Although French violists, playing mainly dance music, placed the thumb on the bow hairs, there is no evidence to show that they regulated the hair tension with it.

During the eighteenth century the bow gradually lengthened, and Tartini is reputed to have instituted the use of lighter wood, fluted at the heel for a surer grip. Some large bows are depicted in the previous century but Hawkins (in his *General History*, 1776) describes the gradual increase in length, over the previous seventy years, to about twenty-eight inches, pointing out that a twenty-four inch bow was known as a 'sonata bow' in 1720 owing to its extra length. Certainly some of the bowings which Tartini recom-

mends to be practised at the point are not playable
there with the length and balance of the modern bow.

The bow was perfected not in Italy, the home of the
violin, but in France, by François Tourte (1747-1835).
After considerable experiment and consultation with
famous violinists (among them Viotti), Tourte settled
on a standard length of 29.1 to 29.3 inches, including
the screw. The diameter of the stick diminished regularly by 0.13 inches over its total length, and he found
that Brazilian pernambuc wood gave the most satisfactory lightness and resilience. The stick was curved
towards the hairs by heat, and the point of balance
brought nearer to the nut (about 19 cm. away from it).
Pre-Tourte bows sometimes appear to have a negative
curve, but the stick usually becomes straight when the
hair is tightened for playing. Tourte may also have
been responsible for attaching the hairs (their number
increased now to between two hundred and two hundred and fifty) in the form of a broad ribbon instead
of a sheath.

The modern technique of bowing has changed considerably since Tourte's type of bow, copied by means
of the rules evolved by his successor, Vuillaume, has
become the standard pattern. So unfamiliar are we
with the qualities of the pre-Tourte bow, that the instructions contained in some eighteenth-century trea-
tises on violin playing have been misinterpreted and
led to a false picture of early violin music. The violin
tutors of Geminiani (1751) and Leopold Mozart
(1756) give detailed instructions about performance,

but these cannot be directly applied to modern bows and instruments.

The pre-Tourte bow has about double the 'give' of the hair of a modern bow : this means that a note will normally begin softly and crescendo to its full strength, unlike the immediate loud attack of the modern bow. A diminuendo towards the point of the old bow was equally inevitable if pace and pressure remained constant, so whereas modern bow technique is based on an even tone throughout the bow, early technique allowed for a basic ＜ ＞ , and as late as Viotti (who used a Tourte bow) a special sign had to be used to indicate equal volume over the whole length of the bow.

Two ways of holding the violin bow were in existence at the beginning of the eighteenth century; one, the French grip, placed the thumb below the hair with three fingers regularly on the stick; the other, which survived longer, was Geminiani's Italian method of inserting the thumb between hair and stick, with four fingers on the stick. Both grips were used quite a distance from the nut: Leopold Mozart's instructions are nearer to the modern idea, as he recommends grasping the bow at the nut and gaining extra pressure from the *second* joint of the index finger, not the first as used by Geminiani.

The pre-Tourte bow left the string most easily at the point, and detached and staccato bowing at the point would sound more clearly separated, but without the hard attack of the modern bow. The smoothness of the modern bow change, making the minimum differentiation between slurred and unslurred bowing on the string, is directly opposed to the effect obtained by the earlier bow, and clarity of enunciation is a more important consideration than smoothness in playing semiquaver passages in eighteenth-century music.

The natural crescendo of the eighteenth-century bow made a quantitative accent on the first of a group of semiquavers or demi-semiquavers a common convention, as the first of a group would otherwise receive a disproportionately small volume of tone. The point of the bow was more frequently used than the heel, judging by contemporary illustration: this, however, does not mean that we should bow most eighteenth-century music at the point, rather the opposite, for whereas the old bow lifted, bounced and separated the strokes most easily towards the point, our bow does these things most easily close to or below the point of balance. Spiccato, played at the point by Tartini, sounds hard and splashy with the modern bow by comparison, unless it is kept below the point of balance, close to the string and away from the bridge. Geminiani condemns staccato with the bow 'taken off the strings at every note', but it should be remembered that owing to the extra give of the hair, his bow could be slightly lifted between notes without leaving the string. Mr. Sol Babitz, who has learned to perform with the eighteenth-century bow and technique (described in *The Score*, March, 1957) gives the following conclusion: 'Modern performers interested in authentic readings would do well to eliminate *all* biting attacks in music before Viotti, and to use very few until after Beethoven'.

The other main question in performing music written for the pre-Tourte bow is that of chordal playing: the modern practice of splitting four-part chords into two and two notes apparently derives from a nineteenth- not an eighteenth-century tradition, and arpeggiation upwards with the lowest note slightly emphasized and played on the beat was the method used in Bach's day and described by Quantz. The eighteenth-century bow was as little capable of sustaining a four-part chord as the modern one, and there is some doubt as to whether the bridge was much less arched than today, as was maintained until recently.

A bow has been invented in this century which is specifically designed for the rendering of Bach's six solo sonatas. By its convexity, and the use of a slightly flatter bridge than usual, four-part chords may be played with all the notes together; and a device for tautening the hairs during performance allows clarity in the monodic passages. This Vega Bach bow, as its main exponent, Emil Telmányi, points out, is not an attempt at reconstructing the conditions of violin playing of Bach's day, but at producing a performance of the sonatas which will reveal most clearly their musical value. Its use, however, presents additional problems of fingering, and it seems doubtful whether violinists will consider the gain in effect worth the effort in acquiring a new style of bow technique which could quite possibly disturb their normal style of playing. Schröder's earlier Bach bow aroused interest but gained few exponents: it was based on Schering's theory (renounced before his death) that the hair tension was controlled by pressing the thumb on the hairs in Bach's time.

The teaching of bowing methods has suffered greatly from the persistence of ill-founded theories and traditions. The inability of the most brilliant and natural performers to analyse their own muscular movements must have been partly responsible for this, another factor being the commonly held fallacy that although the genius may bow one way, the slightly less gifted pupil must practise in the *right* (i.e. traditional) way: he is therefore forced to struggle against additional hindrances such as an immobilized upper arm.

During the last hundred years, certain great performers have possessed and made use of the ability to analyse their technique: through their teaching the modern aim in bowing has become relaxation and the most natural production of sound. Traditions of muscular immobilization, and the over-cultivation of other muscles to compensate, are slow to die, as string technique is passed more through the teacher-pupil relationship than by any writings on the subject. But Pau Casals' example can be said to have instituted internationally a basis of relaxation in cello bowing, and Carl Flesch's observations, carried further by such interesting theses as P. Hodgson's *Motion Study and Violin Bowing*, have gained a wide sphere of influence.

Ševčík has provided several thousand exercises in violin bow technique, but these need to be used sparingly and with a full understanding of the problems they are trying to eliminate: used on the wrong technical basis, they can do more harm than good. Pupils fortunate enough to be trained from the start on principles of relaxation and method of tone production most natural to themselves, without insistence on bowing in straight lines parallel to the bridge, will normally gain an adequate bow technique through the studies of the French school, Fiorillo and Dont.

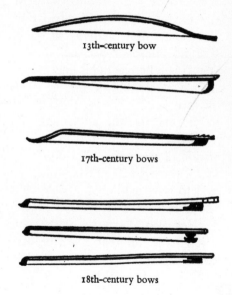

13th-century bow

17th-century bows

18th-century bows

2. PREDECESSORS OF THE MODERN VIOLIN BOW

X. ACOUSTICS OF THE VIOLIN FAMILY

The basic scientific discoveries relating to sound production by vibrating strings may be learned from a book devoted to acoustics: only their practical application to the violin family is relevant here. Remarks concerning the violin in this chapter apply of course to each member of the family.

The first scientific property put to use by the string player is likely to be that if the *length* of a string remains constant, its tension will affect the pitch. In tuning his instrument the violinist is tightening the string to raise its pitch, or slackening it a little to make it lower. When he places his fingers on the string and begins to play a scale, however, he is making use of a different property of vibrating strings; that if the *tension* remains constant, the pitch may be raised or lowered by respectively shortening or lengthening the vibrating portion of the string. A violinist may apply this rule to two, three or four strings simultaneously: he is then said to be using double, triple or quadruple stopping. The thickness and specific gravity of the strings themselves also affect the pitch: considerable experimentation with different types of material has led to a satisfactory standardization of thicknesses in the more expensive strings, although often at the cost of durability.

Apart from these simple string properties, the violinist makes use of a more complex factor: that a string, while vibrating over its whole length, vibrates at the same time in sections which are evenly divisible into the whole—halves, thirds, quarters, fifths, etc.—thus producing the higher notes (given by the shorter lengths) blending in with the fundamental (given by the whole length). The notes produced always bear the same relationship to the fundamental, and are known as the harmonic series. The following are the sounds actually produced, for instance, by bowing the C string of a cello.

Harmonic series

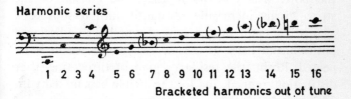

1 2 3 4   5 6   7 8 9 10 11 12 13   14   15 16

Bracketed harmonics out of tune

They are scientifically numbered 1-16 (whereas the string player may refer to the octave harmonic as the first harmonic) and the series contains all intervals. The lowest note is called the fundamental, the upper ones partials or overtones.

The string player unconsciously reproduces the numerical ratios of these intervals when he seeks to play exactly in tune. To raise the pitch by one tone, for instance, (the distance between the eighth and ninth partials) he shortens the string to eight-ninths of its original vibrating length. Similarly, two-thirds of the original length gives a fifth higher: one-half gives the

H

octave. It may be noticed that there are two apparent whole tones in the series, nine : eight and ten : nine. But as each interval in the harmonic series is slightly smaller than the previous one, these tones are not exactly equal, and both have their place in the natural scale (which contains a major (nine : eight) tone followed by a minor (ten : eight) tone within each major third). The violin family has an advantage over keyboard instruments in that these minute discrepancies in pitch may be adjusted to give pure intonation in any key.

In the violin family, the string is set in motion by the bow, which draws it aside, the tension of the string giving increasing resistance until it slips back against the pull of the bow, beyond its undisplaced position and back to normal, when the action is repeated. Rosin (the residuary gum of turpentine after distillation, refined, and for the double bass mixed with white pitch) aids this process by acting as a series of small hooks which drag the string to one side. Bowing gives an advantage over plucked or struck strings in the ability to sustain and to vary the tone of a long note.

The quality of tone produced by normal bowing depends on the strength of the partials, and these are affected by the position of the bow on the string. A very narrow bow would accentuate the shrill upper partials wherever it was used, but the broader bow used with the violin family today gives a more brilliant quality the nearer it is to the bridge, and the amount of hair in contact with the string may be varied to give different effects, by rotating the stick. The extreme bowing positions used (sul tasto to sul ponticello) are from about one-fifth to one-twenty-fifth of the vibrating string length away from the bridge, but the normal place is about one-ninth or one-tenth of the length away, where the dissonant partials are subordinated. The bow is closer to the bridge for the higher left hand positions. In sul ponticello bowing, extra pressure results in the upper partials becoming more prominent than the lower, and a pianissimo tremolo sul ponticello is used as an eerie orchestral effect.

The tone colour is also affected by the method of articulation with the bow, particularly in the initial sound produced, in a way comparable to the initial consonant of a spoken word. This is why the tone of spiccato (jumping) bowing differs from that of normal bowing, as well as the length of note. The difference is caused by the time taken for the note to reach its maximum—in pizzicato and col legno, for instance, the note starts almost immediately; in normal bowing it will take much longer, and varieties of spiccato will come somewhere in between. The ear registers these fractional delays as differences of timbre.

The instruments themselves have a natural tendency to vibrate on notes favoured by their structure. The differences in tone quality between a good and bad violin are usually explained by the extent of these favourable harmonics, a fine instrument reinforcing the higher harmonics fairly evenly, while a poor violin will reinforce lower harmonics with an uneven distribution. An important characteristic of violin tone colour is the difference of quality between different notes, and between the same notes played on different strings. Some notes gain extra fullness from the resonance of parts of the instrument: C or C sharp on the G string of the violin has an added intensity through the resonance of the contained air in the sound-box. 'Wolf notes' are caused by a coincidence of the natural frequency of vibration of a part of the instrument (e.g. the belly) and the string at a certain pitch.

The effect of placing a mute on the bridge is not merely one of softness; it tends to strengthen the fundamental of the lower notes at the expense of the upper partials, and it changes the pitch of wolf notes. It has this profound effect because the bridge is solely responsible for transmitting the string vibrations to the body of the instrument.

It is the left foot of the bridge which is responsible for setting the violin's belly in motion, as the right foot is kept almost still by the sound-post. The vibrations are communicated throughout the wood of the instrument and from the wood to the contained air. It has been found that the upper partials are less intense if the width of the shoulders of the bridge is reduced. Other parts of the instrument's body must be in proportion to the depth of note produced: too small a soundboard (common in small violas) will result in a weak, hollow, nasal tone on low notes.

Other acoustical properties used by the violinist are combination tones (also known as difference tones, resultant tones and Tartini notes), harmonics, and vibrato. Tartini discovered that if high double-stops are played with great intensity exactly in tune, a third tone may be heard below them. This combination tone gives a useful check on intonation when practising, but its practical value is small compared to the other two phenomena.

Harmonics on the members of the violin family are of two types, *natural* (obtained from an unstopped string) and *artificial* (from a stopped string). Scientifically, they are based on the same principle: practically they serve different purposes. Both types are derived from the fact that along a vibrating string are certain points of rest between vibrating sections. These points are called nodes, and they divide the string into a number of equal portions.

Natural harmonics are caused by touching the string lightly at one of the nodes, causing it to vibrate in subsections, by setting up new nodal points. The vibrations occur on both sides of the finger, instead of only above it as in stopped notes.

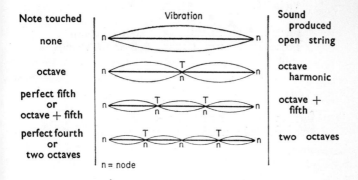

Note touched	Vibration	Sound produced
none		open string
octave		octave harmonic
perfect fifth or octave + fifth		octave + fifth
perfect fourth or two octaves		two octaves

n = node

J

The nodes are equidistant, and the finger may touch any of the points marked T to produce the required harmonic. Theoretically, the string may be caused to vibrate in a great many sub-sections, but in practice only the first six of the harmonic series are used, the seventh being flat and the others too difficult to obtain. The fifth is also a little too flat for most practical purposes.

The normal method of indicating a natural harmonic which sounds at the pitch it is written, is to place 'o' over the note.

Bass (harmonics on fifth string omitted)
N.B. actual pitch

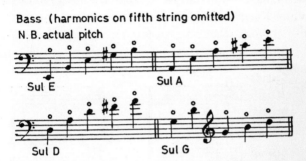

Occasionally, square notes are used although the pitch sounds as written—a misleading practice.

The less common natural harmonics, where the note produced is different from the position of the finger on the string, are indicated by square notes giving the finger position only. The actual sound produced is no longer shown in the music. Square notes are always lightly touched—the smaller and more accurate the area covered, the clearer the harmonic.

The node a minor third above the open string, causing it to vibrate in six sub-sections and therefore producing the sixth note of the harmonic series, is rarely used on the upper strings but more easily obtainable on the bass—an example for the basses is found in bar five of Ravel's *Ma Mère l'Oye*.

The harmonic a major third above the open string (string vibrating in five sub-sections; fifth note of harmonic series) is more common; Ravel uses it on the viola, cello and bass in *Ma Mère l'Oye* and on the violins in *Daphnis and Chloe*, suite 2.

e.g.

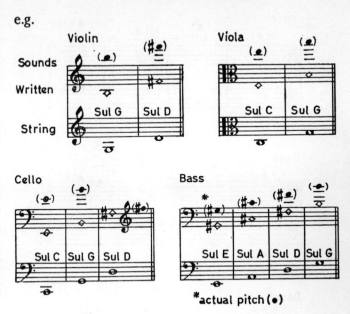

The perfect fourth divides the string into quarters and produces the note two octaves above the open string. Examples are frequent in modern scores; *Ma Mère l'Oye* and *La Valse* of Ravel contain instances.

Viola

Cello

Bass

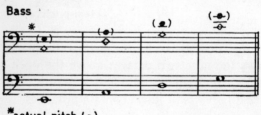

*actual pitch (●)

The node found a perfect fifth above the open string divides the string into three vibrating portions, giving the note a twelfth above the open string. Examples are found in *La Valse* and *Valses Nobles et Sentimentales* of Ravel.

Violin

Sounds

Written

String

Viola

Cello

Bass

*actual pitch (●)

The other natural harmonic found in modern scores (particularly those of Ravel) is produced by lightly touching the major sixth above the open string. This is another node dividing the string into five sub-sections: the note produced is the same as if the major third were touched.

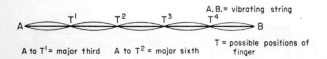

A to T¹ = major third   A to T² = major sixth

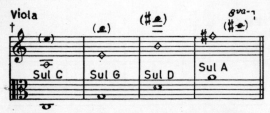

† the square notes would probably be written in the alto clef.

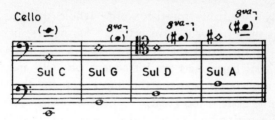

*actual pitch(●)

Double natural harmonics, in fifths (fourths on the bass) appear very occasionally in modern scores. They are produced by touching and bowing two strings simultaneously.

Artificial harmonics are those produced from a stopped instead of an open string. The note is normally stopped by the first finger, and the node touched by the fourth. The number of harmonics obtainable from one length of string is thus limited by the stretch of the hand, but the length of string is easily altered by shifting the hand, giving a far wider range of pitch than the natural harmonics. A complete chromatic scale

from 🎼 upwards for over two octaves is

easily obtainable on the violin; whole melodic passages may be written in artificial harmonics, like the one in the finale of Tchaikovsky's Violin Concerto. Artificial harmonics are infrequent on cello and bass, as the distance between the finger stopping the string and the node is too great.

The major and minor third nodes are possible but very rare in false harmonics; Stravinsky's *Fire-Bird Suite* and Ravel's *Rapsodie Espagnole* contain examples.

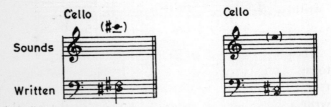

(black note pressed, square note touched in all artificial harmonics)

The node a perfect fourth above the first finger, dividing the vibrating string into quarters and therefore producing a sound two octaves above the note stopped, is by far the most commonly used artificial harmonic on violin and viola. The hand falls in its normal position, the same as that for octaves, and although the whole hand must be shifted for each change in pitch, performers gain enough dexterity at this to make melodic passages possible.

The node a perfect fifth above the stopped note requires a fourth finger extension even on the violin

and viola: it is therefore less use melodically than the
perfect fourth, but appears for isolated notes and when
harmonic tone is required for the notes e flat', f' and f
sharp'.

These are the main harmonics used in string writing
today. Composers do not always indicate clearly the
type of harmonic required, sometimes they merely
write a square note or an ordinary note with 'o', *harm.*,
arm. or *flag.* above it. This can lead to confusion as to
the pitch required.

The use of natural harmonics was known in the
middle ages, for the tromba marina, a curious mediaeval bowed instrument, played only harmonics. The
theory of harmonics was discussed by Mersenne in
1636 and Sauver in 1701, but Mondonville appears to
have been the first to apply the theory to the violin
family, in his sonatas, opus 4 (*c.* 1738). These were
headed *Les Sons harmoniques, sonatas à violon seul, avec
la basse continue.*

Double and false harmonics are usually attributed
to Paganini, who wrote some of the most difficult
harmonic passages, involving very wide stretches of

the hand, in his *Witches' Dances*. Modern composers are still gaining new effects from harmonics col legno (basses, *Fire-Bird Suite*), tremolo (cellos, *ibid*.), pizzicato (Mahler, Symphony No. 9) and glissando (solo violin, *Ma Mère l'Oye*; violas, *Le Sacre du Printemps*) : a glissando to a harmonic has become a fairly common effect in modern scores. Perhaps Debussy and Ravel exploited most successfully the colouring of string harmonics; they are now an accepted extension to the basic range of string pitch and timbre.

Vibrato on stringed instruments is a rapid fluctuation in pitch caused by rocking the finger stopping the string slightly above and below the note alternately. It gives roundness to the tone, and was probably originally copied from the singing voice which develops a natural vibrato. The singing voice has long been the accepted model for instrumentalists; Christopher Simpson in *The Division Violist*, (1659) advocates the use of vibrato in 'any movement of the voice imitated by the viol', and Geminiani, in his violin school (1751) says that 'the art of playing the violin consists in giving that instrument a tone that shall in a manner rival the most perfect human voice'.

Geminiani recommends continuous vibrato, on short notes as well as long: this seems to indicate that the use of some vibrato was an accepted practice before the end of the Baroque era, and not only as an ornament, as in an earlier work he differentiates between occasional ornamental vibrato on the German flute and continuous vibrato on the violin. Until the violin began to be held beneath the chin, however, (this was not a universal practice until the nineteenth century) vibrato must have been difficult to produce: those who doubt this should try to make a continuous vibrato while resting the violin below the collar-bone, the position recommended by Geminiani's violin school.

Mersenne (in his *Harmonie Universelle* 1636) gives one of the earliest clear descriptions of violin vibrato: describing the violin, he says 'Now the beautiful and charming harmonies which may be evoked from it are so numerous, that one may well prefer it to all other instruments, for the strokes of the bow are sometimes so ravishing that one can think of no greater dissatisfaction than to hear the end of them, especially when they are mingled with quiverings and gentle motions of the left hand, which constrain listeners to admit that the violin is a king of instruments.' Leopold Mozart (father of Wolfgang Amadeus, a well-known teacher and composer of Haydn's Toy Symphony!) gives a technical description in his *Violinschule* (1756): '. . . one presses the finger heavily on the string and makes a gentle motion with the entire hand, which, however, must proceed not toward the side but forward toward the bridge and back toward the scroll.'

Today, an almost continuous vibrato is accepted as part of the natural colouring of string tone. Some great artists such as Joachim, Sarasate, Flesch and Auer have pointed out the danger of too much vibrato, and Lionel Tertis advocates a vibrato 'neither too fast, nor

—Heaven forbid!—too slow', adding 'Vital to the expressive use of the vibrato is that it should be continuous: there must be no break at the instant of changing from one note to the other or in the changing of position'. It has been pointed out by Casals and other great performer-teachers that the function of the vibrato is expressive, and to be expressive, it must be varied. A vibrato used solely to render the tone of each note less raucous to the listener has no expressive quality, its expressiveness, says Casals '. . . depends on how it is applied. The vibrato is a means of expressing sensitivity, but it is not proof of it.'

The vibrato is a very personal aspect of string performance, and is often a reflection of the performer's temperament—the calm person, for instance, will tend to produce a slower vibrato. The heightened tension of a platform appearance often causes a speeding up of the vibrato, therefore some performers sound at their best on the concert platform. Heifetz is of the opinion that the vibrato is mainly improved unconsciously through contact with other performers; Isaac Stern and Mischa Elman both stress the importance of varying the vibrato, the former emphasizing the type of vibrato suited to various composers, the latter noting the extra intensity required for the most important notes of a phrase.

Variety of vibrato may be obtained by the use of finger, wrist and arm in different proportions. Primrose and Piatigorsky apply the same principles to the viola and cello as the great violinists to the violin: we may conclude that the vibrato is a very important factor in a fine performance.

Scientific researches into string vibrato have provided the information that the average speed of violin artists is approximately seven vibrato cycles per second, teachers and students using a slightly slower rate. No very wide survey has yet been made; the extremes encountered were 4.5 and 9.5 cycles. The cello student had a quicker vibrato than the artist, who used a slower rate than the violin artist.

The average fluctuation in pitch of string artists was found to be one quarter of a tone, as compared to a semitone in singers. Students and teachers use a smaller extent, and in all performers the extent tends to increase with loudness. Considerable controversy has been aroused over the question of whether one should vibrato below or above the correct pitch. Most string players, when asked, state that they vibrato above the note, yet the definition of vibrato in *Modern Violin Playing* by Grimson and Forsyth as 'a rapid alternation of correct and flattened pitch' is accepted by many people. The scientists' finding is that the middle pitch is heard by the listener: if this is the case, probably all string players with good intonation vibrate equally on either side of the note, differing only in that the initial movement of their cycle is above or below the true pitch. All agree that no fluctuation in pitch must be noticeable, and that the note should begin and end at the correct pitch.

Perhaps vibrato is the most difficult acoustical aspect

of string performance to explain: there are several details of string tone not yet fully understood scientifically. But a logical connection between vibrating strings, columns of air, pitch, frequency and timbre has gradually been discovered. Music used to be counted one of the sciences; and the physics of sound is as important to the musician as to the scientist.

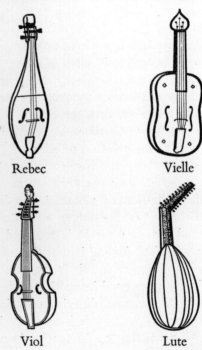

Rebec   Vielle

Viol   Lute

3. EARLY STRINGED INSTRUMENTS SHOWING
DIFFERENT TYPES OF PEG BOX

BOOK LIST

ABELE (trans. Alwyn). 'The Violin and its Story' (1905, *Strad Library* No. 15).

APPLEBAUM, S. & S. *With the Artists* (1955, John Marbert & Co., New York).

BABITZ, S. 'Differences between eighteenth century and modern violin bowing' (*Score*, Mar. 57).

BERLIOZ, H. (trans. Clarke). *Modern Instrumentation and Orchestration* (1838, Novello).

BOYDEN, D. 'The Violin and its technique in the eighteenth century' (*Musical Quarterly*, January, 1950)

BOYDEN, D. 'The Violin and its Technique, New Horizons in Research (*Proceedings of the International Musicological Society*, Cologne, 1958).

CARSE, A. *The Orchestra in the Eighteenth Century* (1940, Heffer and Sons, Cambridge).

DART, T. *The Interpretation of Music* (1954, Hutchinson).

DOLMETSCH, A. *The Interpretation of Music of the XVII and XVIII centuries* (1915, 1944, Novello).

FARGA, F. *Violins and Violinists* (1950, Rockliff).

FLESCH, C. (trans. Martens). *Art of Violin Playing* (Fischer).

FLESCH, C. (trans. Keller). *Memoirs* (1957, Rockliff).

FORSYTH, C. *Orchestration* (1922, Macmillan).

GEIRINGER (trans. Miall). *Musical Instruments* (1945, George Allen and Unwin).

GEMINIANI *The Art of Violin Playing* (1751, Facsimile, Oxford University Press).

HAYES, G. R. *Musical Instruments* 1500-1750 (1930, O.U.P.).

HODGSON, P. 'Motion Study and Violin Bowing' (1934, *The Strad*.).

HYATT-KING, A. *Chamber Music* (1948, Max Parrish).

JALOVEC, K. *Italian Violin Makers* (1952, Orbis).

JEANS, J. *Science and Music* (1937, Cambridge University Press).

LELAND 'The Dounis Principles of Violin Playing' (1949, *The Strad*).

LOWERY, H. *A Guide to Musical Acoustics* (1956, Dobson).

MEYER, E. *English Chamber Music* (1945, Lawrence and Wishart).

MOZART, L. (trans. Knocker). *Violin Playing* (1756, 1948, O.U.P.).

PANUM, H. *Stringed Instruments of the Middle Ages* (Reeves).

PINCHERLE, M. 'Corelli' (1933, *Librairie Felix Alcan*).

PINCHERLE, M. *Les Violonistes*.

PINCHERLE, M. (trans. Hatch). *Vivaldi* (1958, Gollancz).

ROBERTSON, A. (ed.). *Chamber Music* (1957, Penguin Books).

ROWEN, R. H. *Early Chamber Music* (1949, King's Crown Press N.Y.).

SACHS, C. *History of Musical Instruments* (1942, Dent).

SANDYS AND FORSTER *The Violin* (1864, John Russell Smith).

SEASHORE, C. (ed.). *The Vibrato* (1952, University of Iowa).

STRAETEN, VAN DER. *The History of the Violin* (1933).

TERTIS, L. *Cinderella No More* (1953, Peter Nevill).

VEINUS, A. *The Concerto* (1948, Cassell).

WOOD, A. *The Physical Basis of Music* (1913, 1944 Methuen).

INDEX